The Lily and The Moon

Train yourself in the ideal of the lily, which blossoms in the mud and has to keep itself engaged in the struggle for existence day in and day out, parrying, bracing, and fighting the shocks of muddy water and storms and squalls and sundry other vicissitudes of fortune, and yet it does not forget the moon above. It keeps its love for the moon constantly alive. It seems, however, but a most ordinary flower. There is nothing extraordinary about it. Still this most ordinary little flower has a romantic tie with the great moon. Similarly, you may be an ordinary creature -- you may have to pass your days in the ups and downs of your worldly existence -- still do not forget that Supreme One. Keep all your desires inclined towards Him. Always keep yourselves merged in His thought. Go deep into the mood of that Infinite Love.

Most of these discourses were translated from the original Hindi or Bengali. In this version some adjustments have been made in the original translations for the sake of clarity.

Those interested in learning more about Ánanda Márga, its service work or meditation teachings, may contact: 854 Pearl Street, Denver, Colorado 80203

First Printing July 1973
Second Printing December 1973

ISBN 0-88476-001-4
Copyright © 1973 AMRIT PUBLICATIONS of ÁNANDA MÁRGA

Published by ÁNANDA MÁRGA PUBLICATIONS, 27160 Moody Road, Los Altos Hills, California 94022 U.S.A. Telephone [415] 948-9841. Type set at American Publishing, Inc. Santa Clara, California, Printed at Braun-Brumfield, Ann Arbor, Michigan.

BÁBÁ'S GRACE

Discourses of Shrii Shrii Ánandamúrti

SHRII SHRII ÁNANDAMÚRTI is the spiritual guide for millions of spiritual aspirants all over the world. He is called Bábá, which means "beloved". From His early childhood, men and women of all ages have been drawn to Him by the power of His love. Living an ordinary life, as a child, as a schoolboy, as a railway officer in a small town in India, at the same time He taught many sincere seekers how to realize the Truth within themselves. Soon the number of His disciples was multiplying so rapidly that He began to train others to teach the practices of self-realization; and thus the organization *Ananda Márga*, the Path of Bliss, was founded, and spread rapidly all over the world.

Those who follow His teachings find their lives transformed; the confining walls of their egos dissolve and an all-embracing cosmic feeling begins to fill their hearts. They begin to look on all people as brothers and sisters, as the manifestations of the Supreme. They want to serve those manifestations. They cannot bear to see others in pain, and they want to share with all the bliss which they themselves enjoy. From Hong Kong to Buenos Aires to New York, many people are working tirelessly in the service of humanity, motivated by His indescribable love.

In these discourses Bábá speaks of the journey of the Soul. The journey begins with Absolute Consciousness, the pure essence, *Paramapuruśa*, God. Due to the force of the Cosmic Energy, *Prakrti*, that Supreme Essence is transformed into this vibrational, manifested world, into "crude" matter. And then the return journey home begins. The creation, drawn by that supreme attractive force of the Cosmic Nucleus -- the power of love -- gradually evolves again into subtler and subtler entities, with higher and higher expressions of consciousness: unicellular organisms, plants, animals, higher animals, and finally man, the most evolved manifestation of that Consciousness.

At a certain point in his evolution, there awakens inside of man a desire to know himself, to know his purpose in life. When this desire awakens, he is ready to begin *sádhana*, the "effort of completion," the practices of meditation by which he will accelerate his evolution and hasten his journey home to the pure Consciousness from which he came. When this desire awakens in him, his guide appears, the teacher who will lead him forward on the path of realization. *Guru* means "dispeller of darkness," and the Master does exactly that; with His own divine powers, He clears the clouds from His beloved disciples' minds. He helps them transcend all their negative tendencies so that their true nature -- divine perfection -- may shine forth from within. For the *Guru* is verily the perfect expression of that Supreme Consciousness. It is God who in the form of the *Guru* is drawing His beloved children to Himself. As the disciple progresses more and more on the path of realization, as his perfect nature flowers more and more within him, he feels the pervasiveness of love -- God's love, the *Guru*'s love, love within himself -- and in ecstasy he sees love everywhere. God, the *Guru*, his innermost self, and all creation, all become one.

The devotee reaches this sublime state by His Grace alone. For the devotee, His Grace is all.

CONTENTS

The Lord's Play	13
Man and His God	16
Returning Home	22
The Pond and The Pot	26
Rudra	28
Madhúvidya: Honey Knowledge	37
God and His Creation	40
The True Devotee	58
The Ocean of Grace	60
Service	64
Shelter to the Sinners Also	70
The Lord's Palms	73
The Divine Will	76
Knowledge, Action, & Devotion: Jiṋána, Karma & Bhakti	80
Live According to God's Desire	85
Offering of Colors	88
Dagdhabiija	91
Paramapuruśa	94
Occult Powers or Paramapuruśa?	106

The Lord's Grace is All	110
God is With You	112
Knowledge	123
Pride and Its Cure	125
Longing for the Great	130
The Highest Devotee	138
One and Zero	139
Bhakti: Devotion	141
The Mission of Being Perfect	150
Taking Refuge at His Feet	152
The Lord's Feet	155
Virtue and Vice	159
God	166
The Essence of Spirituality	169
The Sound of God	172
Desire and Devotion	175
The Clarion Call of the Universal	187
Departing Message from the Philippines	188
Surrender	189
Glossary	193

THE LORD'S PLAY

There is a Single Entity, a Single Personality in this universe. Apparently you are many, but fundamentally you are one. The One is manifest in many. The creation of this universe, its substance is One, though creation is manifold. Why this creation of One into many? The reply is only with the Creator, the Supreme Lord. Philosophers try to answer this question but fail. How far can a microcosmic brain with its small nerve fibres go? Even if he utilizes all his mental powers he cannot succeed. The devotee's approach to this question is, however, different. He enters God's mind, mingles his mind with that of the Supreme Being and knows some of the secrets of God's mind from within.

The devotees say God is supreme. They sing His glory and defend all His actions. That is why God says, "My devotees are greater than Myself."

The common man says, "O God, we are tired of Your *liilá*. What is the need of it? We are all suffering and You call it Your play."

The devotee, however, defends God thus: "My Lord was utterly alone before the creation. A man becomes mad if he is alone for a long time in a big vacant house. God was restless before creation. He could neither love nor feel angry with anyone. So creation was a compulsion. He has created all these forms by multiplying Himself. When God was alone, He had the power to see, but there were no objects to be seen. Now that He has started creation, He sees whatever He thinks. If we who are His own forms feel a little restlessness in His creation, we are blessed for we are saving our Lord from the restlessness of utter loneliness."

This is the way a devotee looks at the secret of creation. We are all part of that Supreme Being -- He is playing with Himself in all our forms. This is a divine play. He is playing hide-and-seek with Himself. Search Him in your little "I-feeling" and you will find the King of kings there. In fact, the name of this search is *sádhana*.

If you do not go within, do you want to go out? But where will you go, since He is everywhere in this universe, and surrounding this universe?

You cannot go outside Him. He is there within and without -- in your small "I" as well as in this big universe. He alone is a Single Entity pervading all forms.

By thinking of Him one becomes free from all kinds of bondages like fear, etc., and one who is free from bondages is He Himself. Knowing Him is being Him. This is the way of establishing oneself in Him -- becoming the Single Entity by transcending the many forms.

Doing *sádhana*, becoming one with this Single Entity, is your birthright, which no one can take away from you. Kick all obstacles from your path of becoming one with Him. Do not feel afraid of anybody. The Lord is with you. He will guide you forward. Victory is yours. O

MAN AND HIS GOD

The *Yogi* says there is hardly any difference between the terms, "God" and "Bliss." They are just like the two names, "water and "aqua," used for the same entity. The *Yogi* says, "What is God? He is Bliss. He is *Ánanda*." Everything comes from Him, remains in Him, and goes back to that Supreme Entity. And what is that Supreme Entity? It is *Ánanda*, bliss.

God is the Generator, He is the Operator, and He is the benevolent Destructor. G.O.D. What is God? As operator, He is the controller also. The operator of the machine must have control over that machine. He must be a controller. And this controller is not only an ordinary mechanic, but He is a great Magician because He creates everything in His mind. The magician creates so many things in his mind and the spectators say, "Oh, he is a great magician." But actually these spectators are befooled. Their minds go towards that created object and not towards the magician. But they should know that these created items are of temporary nature; the magician is the truth. So this controller is a great

Magician. He is creating everything within His mind. All the created beings are within His mind. And for those created beings, the mental world of this Magician appears to be a physical one.

Suppose you create a candle in your mind and a man in your mind. You know that both the candle and the man are mental creations; they are purely mental, not physical. They are within your mind. But for your mental man, your mental candle is a reality. Similarly, for you this world is a physical reality. But for that Supreme Magician, everything is mental. Everything is transitory. He is a magician and He has control over the entire universe.

Now what is God again? The *Yogi* says, "He who has occult powers, all the occult powers, all the occult faculties, is God." Unless and until one possesses all the occult powers, how can one control the universe?

The occult powers are eight in number. He who is the owner of all these occult powers is known as *Iishvara* in Sanskrit. And why is God called *Iishvara?* He can see everything. He can go to any place without the help of any organ.

Another explanation of the *Yogi* to the question "Who is God?" is, "He who remains unassailed, unaffected by the actions and reactions is God. He who requires no shelter. He who is the shelter of all, of everything. He is God."

Another explanation of the *Yogi* is that the universe is a collection of so many electrons, protons, positrons, etc. and He who is the Supreme Controller of all of them is God. You have only two eyes, and those eyes can function only where there are light waves in the external world. Where light waves are lacking you cannot see. But He has infinite eyes and all His eyes are functioning within because there is nothing outside Him. Everything is within Him. In order to see your mental pictures, do you depend upon external eyes? No. For you there are two worlds, internal and external. But in His case, everything is internal. You are within His mind, and whatever you are seeing, whatever you are doing, whatever you are going to do, everything is being done within His great mind. There is nothing external. He says "Oh My child, oh My real child. Why did you commit such a sin?" You can't say, "No, Father, I didn't commit a sin," because you are in His mind. He sees internally without the help of any eyes, because you are His mental creation, you are within His mind.

He is omnipresent, He is everywhere. The movement of a grain of sand is as important to Him as the movement of an atom bomb, as the movement of a megaton bomb. For Him nothing is unimportant. You cannot be unimportant for Him. The Supreme Father is always with you. And because of His omnipresence, there is one advantage and one disadvantage. What is the advantage? The advantage is, the Supreme Father is always with you, you are never alone. You must not be afraid of anybody, because He is always waiting to save you. And the disadvantage is that He is always with you. And that's why it is very difficult for you to do anything undesirable, anything unpleasant. This is the difficulty. The universe is being surrounded by Him. Whatever you do, your doing is being witnessed by Him. You cannot think secretly.

Máyá is the force which creates the illusion of this physical reality. It is the Operative Principle of God. Now this *Máyá* is insurmountable for an ordinary man, for a non-*sádhaka* [non-spiritual aspirant]. A man who is not a spiritual aspirant, has to serve the *Máyá* as a slave. This is the case with all animals, with all brutes, and people of animal temperament. Now what is the purpose of intuitional practices, of *Yogic* practice? It is just to overcome the influence of this *Máyá*. This Operative Principle, the influence of *Máyá*, is just like a satanic chain, just like a serpentine noose of affliction and predicaments. One has to free oneself from this serpentine noose. And this is done by *Yogic sádhana* [meditation]. When the *Yogi* comes in close contact with the Supreme Father, the Lord says, "Oh my boy, it is very difficult for a man to overcome the influence of this *Máyá*. This *Máyá* is insurmountable. But he who has taken shelter in Me, he who has ensconsed himself in Me, he who has taken shelter on My lap, he will surely go beyond the influence of this *Máyá*."

Unless and until you have developed implicit faith and sincere love for that Supreme Father, you will not become one with Him, you will be bound to this *Máyá*. Now when does a man feel that he should love the Lord? When he frees himself from evil, from egoistic sentiments. But he will say, "They say God is gracious, but I am an unfortunate fellow, I am not realizing His grace." There are many persons who talk like this, but you know, my sons, you know, my daughters, there is no partiality in Him. His heavenly shower of grace is for all. He is for each and every creature, but one feels His Grace while another does not. What is the reason? There is a heavenly shower of grace. But suppose you are holding an umbrella over your head. Will you be drenched by the shower? Oh no. He who wants to enjoy this shower of grace must remove the umbrella of ego from his head, and he will be drenched by the divine shower. So a spiritual aspirant, a *Yogi*, must give up all his egoistic sentiments. And in the next moment he will be in the proximity of the Supreme Father. ○

*Is He moving?
No, no, He is not. He lies
motionless like the stump of the
tree. Is He far away? No, no, He is
not. He is very close. He is the Life of my
life. He is within you, within me. He is
within and without all and at all places.
When a sádhaka gets adequately acquainted
with His Blissful Entity, we say that he is
established in God. At that stage both inside
and outside attain unity. Mind then remains
aloof from the attraction of trifles, and real
acquaintance is made with the Supreme
Being. While the body remains in the
mortal world, the soul is merged
in the Supreme Soul.*

RETURNING HOME

In simple words, what we have to do is to return home from where we came. We have all come from the Supreme Entity, the Nucleus of the Universe. We have to return to the same destination. The boy has played throughout the day away in the fields and now that evening has come, he returns home. *Sádhana* therefore is the process of returning home.

The child has played outside for the whole day. As evening approaches he thinks that his father must have returned home. "Let me return home and sit near him," he thinks. When one is tired of this world and of worldliness, he yearns to go back to spirituality -- his home. And what is our permanent abode? It is the Supreme Father, the Supreme Consciousness. Therefore going home is a simple task. It requires no scholarship, no knowledge, no intellectual faculty, no long and tedious lecturing. The scriptures say that there are three points to remember for returning home. They are hearing the name of the Lord, thinking only about God and about none else, and offering one's mind to God.

The importance of hearing the name of God in spiritual development is great. Hearing about God is much more important in spirituality than studies, since sound is subtler. Therefore, whenever there is an opportunity, listen to His name and tell it to others. Whenever you tell His Name to others, you also hear it. This dual enjoyment of the recitation of His name is called *kiirtan* [chanting the Lord's name]. *Bhajan* [singing devotional songs], on the other hand, is hearing His name by oneself. You must do both -- *bhajan* as well as *kiirtan*. This is *shravana* [hearing].

Thereafter comes *manana*, that is, thinking only about God and about none else. If any other person or thing comes in the mind, ascribe Godhood to that person or thing. This process is *manana*.

Now what is left over is the "I-hood", the ego. We have to wipe out this "I-hood". All burdens, all confusions, all considerations of respect or disrespect are connected with this "I". When someone does not agree with you, you file a suit in the court. Why do you take such trouble? Only to vindicate your ego. All troubles and frustrations are solely due to the unit ego. The fact is that even after surrendering everything to God, the arch enemy, the "I", remains. You will say, "I have surrendered everything to God" -- I, I, I! My friend, surrender this "I" also to God and then alone your surrender will be complete. All the trouble is due to this "I".

Really speaking, the only task to be performed is to give away everything to God. All that you possess -- your body, your name, fame, wealth, everything -- you have received from God. Then what are you to give Him and how are you to do it? So far you were only giving God's things back to Him. What you have to give Him is something of your own. This is the crux of the matter. Someone gives you a flower as a gift and you return the same flower to him. This is not proper. Why not give Him your "I", which is the source of all your troubles, all your confusions, all your complications? There is nothing dearer to you than this "I". It is most difficult to give it up. Thus exclaims the devotee, "O God, this universe is Your abode. It is full of precious jewels. Whatever there is of value in this world belongs to You. Then what precious gift can I give You? You have no need for any of these. What is the use of offering anything to one whose house is full of precious jewels? The almighty *Prakrti* [Cosmic Energy] is Your own consort. At Your will she will make innumerable jewels in a moment -- the dexterous hand of this Creative Power is ever-ready to serve You. O Lord of Lords, although I yearn to offer You something, I do not know what that thing should be. Although I want to offer, You have no desire or want. When You lack nothing what can I offer? If I could know something that you do not possess, I would offer it to You.

"O Lord of Lords, we hear that Your great devotees have snatched your mind from You. God becomes the slave of His devotees. The devotee steals the heart of God -- almost forcibly. It is performed openly and not in secret. Then O Lord, you lack one thing -- you have no mind." The devotee says, "Despair not, O Lord, I am offering my mind to You. Please accept it." This offer of one's mind to God is complete surrender. Complete surrender makes it possible to merge with the Supreme Entity. This is God-realization.

When you come in close contact with the Supreme Entity you will find that you have no other wealth superior to devotion. All other worldly possessions prove of no avail. Only devotion enables you to have close contact with Him. This is the goal of human life. This is true progress. You have been wandering through the labyrinth of myriad lives and advancing forward to attain this stage. Knowingly or unknowingly you are being drawn unto Him. Here is the summum bonum of life. As long as you do not realize Him there is no success in your life. ○

THE POND AND THE POT

So now you understand that as long as you crave your own selfish happiness, the happiness of the Cosmic touch will continue to elude you. Take your petty "I" with all its pettiness toward the Great -- enlarge and broaden it. Be one with that Sublime Entity and then alone can you really attain Him. When your entire entity is saturated through and through with the nectar of Cosmic Bliss, can your existence then remain separate?

Now the question arises: will man give up all his secular occupations after the attainment of *Brahmic* [spiritual] happiness? Why should he? The man whose life is saturated with the nectar of Cosmic Bliss will go on doing more efficiently and more beautifully all secular works as the cherished assignment of God Himself. He will not bother about his own happiness or pleasure in any work. For the collective happiness of the universe he will go on doing every work properly and flawlessly -- the collectivity of the universe is the Life of his life, the Soul of his soul, God. He will use his insignificant ego as an aid for the happiness of the Great Ego.

And what is the result? A spiritual aspirant, forgetting his own happiness and sorrow, goes on doing the desired works of *Brahma*. He does not want anything for himself; he wants only to give Him happiness. But strange are the ways of God! As the result of such selfless love the *sádhaka* himself tastes an inexhaustible happiness and feels himself fortunate. He feels in his heart of hearts how valued even his insignificant ego is, as a tool of His Grace.

In order to realize the Supreme Perfection man will have to give up his "I-ness"; that is to say, he will have to merge his petty "I-feeling" in the Great "I-feeling". What is this petty "I"? It is like a pot full of water in a pond. Now, if the water of the pot is to be unified with that of the pond -- actually both the waters are intrinsically one -- the pot intervening between the two waters has to be removed. After the removal of the pot, there will remain no distinction between the water of the pot and the water of the pond -- both become one.

The cause of this apparent distinction between God and the unit, is this pot -- the individual mind.

The long and short of the whole thing is that He is infinite. If you want to realize His characteristic Self, you have to earn limitlessness yourself. ○

RUDRA

Every living being belongs to the family of the Supreme Being, *Rudra*. Where there is one Supreme Father, how can there be different castes and creeds? You are all equal; none is inferior and none is superior. Those who create distinctions are the enemies of human society. Fundamentally you are all one and only apparently you are many. *Rudra* is the final substance of all beings.

Why call the Supreme Being "*Rudra*"? The word *Rudra* in Sanskrit means "weeping." But the Supreme Being not only makes all weep, He also makes them laugh! In both the circumstances, that is, of extreme pain and pleasure, there are tears in the eyes. In pain the tears come from the middle of the eyes, in pleasure they come from the corners of the eyes. A mother weeps when her daughter goes to her in-laws' house. She also weeps when her daughter returns from the house of her in-laws. In one case she weeps for pain, in another she weeps for joy.

If living beings were to live in one state always, there would be extreme monotony and no one would want to continue life. If in a drama we know the end in the very beginning, there would be no interest in the play. We need suspense, ups-and-downs and eleventh-hour surprises to keep life interesting. God, that is, *Rudra*, is a first-class dramatist. He keeps life floating within the two extremes of joy and pain; hence His *liilá*, His play, goes on.

We pray to *Rudra* in the following way: "O Lord! take me from the transitory to the eternal!!" All forms are momentary; only God is changeless, *sat*, truth. Therefore take me from *asat*, the transitory, to *sat*, truth.

"O Lord! Guide us from darkness unto light!" Darkness here means *Máyá* or ignorance which creates confusion about reality. When this *Máyá* is removed, the individual soul becomes the Universal Soul.

"O Lord! Take me from death unto life!" Death simply means change. In this created universe all will change and all are changing. Thus everything, every being is subject to death. Save me from this realm of death and make me a non-changing absolute, which alone is immortality.

"O Lord *Rudra*, you are manifested in all things and forms; I want to feel your presence in my heart!"

Sádhakas [spiritual aspirants] will get this feeling with the slightest effort. You people will complete your mission here and in this life, so that we may all take up another mission on some other planets!

Rudra is *Guru* [dispeller of darkness], father and teacher all rolled into one.

Rudra is described as having five faces. What do these indicate? *Rudra* is one, but has five types of administrative functions. Everyone has his duty. The Supreme Being, also having manifested Himself into relativity, has His duties. He works hard for His mundane beings, who are His children.

The face to the extreme right is called *Dakśińeshvara*. Its role is to tell the human beings, "Please my child, do not do this -- I shall be pained if you do this." This is a gentle warning to prevent evil.

The face on the extreme left is called *Vámadeva*. It says, "Why did you do this? I shall smash you." It actually punishes and destroys.

The next face to the extreme right is *Iisháná*. It says, "Do not do this, you may get punishment for this." It is mildly rebuking but not threatening.

The face next to the extreme left is *Kálagni*. It threatens severely but does not actually punish.

In the middle is the face of extreme serenity and beauty. It is called *Kalyān Sundaram*. Suppose there is a child of 3-4 months. Both the parents look at him with great affection. There is no desire to punish at all. This central face of the *Rudra* is His permanent nature. It is the quality of grace and beauty which is the only lasting characteristic and property of *Rudra*. Changes in this to the right or left are only due to administrative requirements.

The devotees pray to *Rudra*, "O Lord, kindly look at me with your extreme right face so that I may be prevented from evil and hence punishment."

But God is one and always graceful and kind. The concept of God and devil co-existing is neither logical nor practical. There cannot be two rival powers contending for superiority. The destructive aspects of God are also due to His extreme kindness towards His creation. When a shirt is torn and you change it for a new one, it is not an act of cruelty. God creates this universe, maintains it and goes on destroying its useless parts or changing them for new ones. *Rudra*, being the final power in this universe, also has final responsibility to protect, maintain and control it. Power and responsibility should go hand in hand.

When He finds a particular structure incapable of performing its part well, He discards it for another. It is like the organizer of a puppet show changing one of His puppets. Therefore in His destroying aspect also, God is not to be feared. He is only to be loved.

There is going to be no final destruction of this creation. But suppose this were going to happen, even then the human beings need not be afraid, as they will remain on the lap of *Rudra* even in that state. So no one should feel afraid. The word "fear" should be removed from the dictionary of mankind.

Do not think that because you are small or uneducated, God will not attend to you. He bestows the same measure of care for the biggest elephant as He does for the smallest ant. For Him both are one and the same -- His progeny. If no one else thinks of you, do not worry, *Rudra* will think about you.

The more inward you go in your mind, the nearer you are to *Rudra*. Finally when your mind merges in its source, you are one with *Rudra*. You have immense possibilities; the Supreme Being, the Supreme Power is within your easy reach. Why then fear anyone?

The sweetest part of *liilá* -- God's play -- is that He is hidden in everyone and everyone is searching for him. He wants His children to go round and He plays hide-and-seek with them. This is so that they may perform certain essential functions in the process. This gives interest and pleasure to both the Creator and the created.

Thus all things are one. There is no distinction due to sex, age, or anything. Male and female, young and old are all actors playing different roles in the drama of this universe. Their forms differ, but their substance and purpose is one. God is male, female, child, youth, and old age.

God has His faces in all directions. No one can hide anything from Him. He sees both our external and internal actions. Do not hate those who are small. You have no right to hate anyone. Do not be afraid of nature either. The thunder and the roar of the oceans hide His sweet music within their apparently frightful sounds. Fear none and hate none. All are One.

This Universal Form of God, Unity in all -- you will be able to see in this very life. Strive on -- go on doing your *sádhana* intensively, you will succeed.

Movement is life. Where this is towards God, the Subtle, the All in One -- it is progress, otherwise it is degradation. The moment a man is born he starts his journey. The end of his journey is death. The gap between these two is life. It is a small gap. Waste no time. Every minute takes you nearer to the grave. There is no time to waste. This mission of life -- to be one with God -- has to be fulfilled here and now.

The mind also moves and changes, but it has no relation with this body and its grave. Bodies are given up one by one, but the mind remains the same continuing unit.

All creation is dancing round the *Paramapuruśa*, whether knowingly or otherwise. The steps and the direction of one's dance are according to one's nature. Those who are becoming degraded are dancing away from Him. Others are expanding and moving towards Him. This dance is the cycle of *Brahma* [*Brahmacakra*].

Every mind is dominated by one particular desire. Some pray to God, "Please remove my stomach-ache." Others say, "If my daughters get married I shall leave the world and come to You." God smiles at these prayers in silence, as laughing openly would embarrass His children.

Every body and mind is structured according to its dominant desire. You can recognize a good man by his face. People with the same dominant desire easily become friends though they may belong to different countries of the world.

This dance of individuals according to their desire is *rasalülā* or the play of the waves in God's Ocean. As a boat goes up and down on a wave, so the human beings go up and down on the Cosmic waves of their desires. As long as one considers oneself separate from the Lord, this dual dance goes on. When one knows the Supreme Being, the rhythm changes and becomes soothing and graceful.

But coming to know Him is only possible through His Grace. Scholarship will not lead you to God. A devotee will always win when there is a conflict with a scholar. The scriptures are like curd which is churned by scholars -- while they analyze the butter and buttermilk, the butter is eaten up by the devotees and only stale buttermilk is left for the scholars.

How to get this kindness, this Grace from God? You have to snatch it from Him, just as a little child by weeping bitterly snatches his mother's love and attention, though the mother at first may be unwilling to leave the kitchen for the child.

But the devotees always plead for God. They justify His actions. They say, we are doing our *sádhana* not to get pleasure but to please our Lord. He feels happy when He sees His creation making attempts to meet Him.

God's Grace is forever raining over all but we keep umbrellas of our ego aloft and hence do not get drenched in it. Devotees, however, puncture this ego. They surrender themselves to Him and thus get His Grace.

Since all beings have come out of *Rudra*, He is also their final Goal; merging in God is as natural as being born. *Sádhakas* will surely achieve this. Go on doing your part. I shall do mine and help you in establishing yourself in the Supreme. I have come on this earth for this sake.

If someone wants to inject an inferiority complex in you, do not be affected. You are the children of God, not inferior to anyone. Make attempts to meet Him and success will surely be yours.

Victory is yours. You are the dear ones of God. Move on and achieve the Goal. ○

MADHÚVIDYA: HONEY KNOWLEDGE

The knowledge of God cannot be attained by reading books alone. It needs earnestness, it needs spiritual practice; that is to say, one has to pursue one's path with *Brahma* as the destination. If all tendencies are inclined towards Him, they will become subtler and subtler and will ultimately merge in Him. When there are no tendencies there is no mind. You will go beyond the access of the mind. You will be released from the feelings of pain and pleasure and will ultimately attain the Self.

One has to advance with full endeavor, keeping the mind scrupulously away from vices. Never let your mind's purity be polluted in any way. After practising this for a while, you will observe that the very mind that was the sustainer of your vile tendencies has become your greatest friend. All your purposes will then be served by your mind. Let it have constant inspiration from your Soul. Enlighten your mind with the refulgence of the Soul. The Absolute Truth will reveal Itself in you automatically.

> *Life is a spiritual sádhana, and the result is to be offered at the altar of the Almighty.*

Those who adopt the reverse course are really ignorant, in that by dedicating themselves to a crude object, they transform their mind gradually into crudeness. By gradual degeneration, their mindstuff reaches a stage where they do not even merit to be called human beings. Do not, therefore, dedicate yourself to crude objects. Do not permit yourself to be carried away beyond yourself by impulses and tendencies. Extroverted tendencies and dedication to crude objects are sure impediments to the realization of Self.

But in mundane life, finite objects are indispensable. The preservation of existence cannot be possible by always pursuing the path of *shreya* [spiritual gain] alone. When it is settled that *shreya* alone is necessary for one's supreme spiritual progress, only *shreya* shall have to be pursued, and not *preya* [material gain].

Then the question arises, how will the aspirant maintain his existence during the period of spiritual practices, when he cannot be advised to pursue *preya* of any sort? Therefore, he will have to deal with *preya* in such a manner that it may not become a cause of his bondage or of extroversion of tendencies, but rather lead him to the introversion of tendencies and thereby to *mukti* [liberation]. This skill is known as *madhuvidyá* [honey knowledge].

Madhuvidyá teaches you that you can endeavor to attain *mukti* even while leading a worldly life, provided, of course, that before dealing with any object of gratification you take it with Cosmic feeling. While feeding your son, you ought to contemplate that you are not feeding your son, but are feeding the manifestation of *Brahma* in the shape of your son. When you plough your land, you ought to contemplate that you are serving the manifestation of *Brahma* in the shape of your land. If you properly follow *madhuvidyá* you can keep yourself aloof from the shackles of actions even though you perform actions. This *madhuvidyá* will pervade your exterior and interior being with the ecstasy of the bliss of *Brahma*. This bliss will permanently alleviate all your afflictions. Then *avidyá* [the force leading toward crudeness] cannot come with its ferocious jaws wide open to devour you. The glory of the One and only One Benign Entity will shine forth to you from one and all objects. ○

GOD AND HIS CREATION

It is said that there is a fundamental difference between God and man, between the Creator and His creation. The basic difference is that God is free from all bondages, whereas man is shackled in bondages. The difference between one material object and another is known by their respective qualities. A mango is a mango by virtue of its qualities; an apple is an apple because of its own characteristics. If the characteristics and qualities of the mango come into the apple, then the latter would no longer remain an apple but would become a mango. The difference in the characteristics of the Creator and the created being is what keeps them distinctly separate. If through *sádhana* the created being develops the characteristics of the Supreme Progenitor, then he becomes the Supreme Himself.

Let me say a word about the qualities of God and His created beings. Etymologically, *Iishvara* [a Sanskrit name for God] means "the Controller." God is the Controller, and the living being is the controlled. In this world every object, big or small, from the atom to the cosmos, is controlled by the Supreme Controller. In the physical realm, you are not the controller of every action. Man does not know that he might die the next moment. He is controlled by Someone who has the absolute right to do so. And He cannot be questioned. When the landlord wants his tenant to vacate his house, he serves the latter a notice. What can the tenant do? He can at best take the help of the law.

Now, you do not even own your body. You can only use it. God is its owner. If He wants, He can take back your body, and He can do it without even serving you a notice. In the realm of God there are no legal courts. He is the Supreme Owner and His right is absolute, perenially absolute. God is the controller and the controlled beings cannot say anything; they will have to surrender to Him.

So you have seen the relation between God and the created beings! God has the control in His hands and the living beings are not free. Of course, you can say that in the reign of God there is a certain measure of liberty. If you stoop to condemn God, He will not say anything. But do you realize that you are able to vilify God only through His power? You take power from God to vilify Him! Now what will you do when God is the Controller? This controlling power of God is wondrous and even magical. The magician converts a stone into a pigeon and the people only watch the transformation. How the stone got transformed into the pigeon, this the people do not understand. Did it actually get transformed or not -- this the people do not know. The mystery behind it is known only to the magician and the few men of his party who are on the stage with him.

God is controlling everyone by His magical power. What will the person who wants to ferret out the inner secrets of God's magical power do? To know the what and why and how of God's magical influence, you will have to go into the fold of the Master Magician's party and develop love for Him. By loving, and not quarreling with the Supreme, and by being in His fold, you will know the secret technique of His control. How can man move forward on the path of progress? By developing love for God.

Maharishi Kanad, a great saint, used to ask what this cosmos is. The universe is the combination of atoms. An atom is a material force, a crude force, a physical force. If the activities of the world are left to the atom, what would happen? There would be clash and struggle! If the atom were everything, this beautiful, evolved and systematic world that works on certain rules and principles, would not be found. *Maharishi Kanad* said that elementary matter exists, but matter does not control matter. What controls it is the cognitive faculty -- God. Blind force cannot create a systematic world. You have to save yourself from the serpentine noose of materialism, and you can save yourself by surrendering to God. The man who expeditiously surrenders to God is wise, and his progress will be tremendously fast.

Man is not merely the crude physical body with hands and legs: man is bigger and greater than this. The physical body is not controlled by the body but by the mind, which in turn is controlled by the unit consciousness. And unit consciousness is controlled by Cosmic Consciousness [God]. Therefore, the wise man will move according to the desire of God. Motivated according to God's desire, man will engage in the activities of the world.

What is the other characteristic of God? He remains unaffected or unconcerned by anguish, action, reaction and dependence. All the creatures in this world do not have the same standard of elevation. If man continues to elevate his mind until it reaches beyond the periphery of these four things, then he becomes God.

Now what is anguish? That which impairs the naturalness of the mind -- that state which a man wants to avoid -- is called anguish. Suppose you smell something fetid. Your mind will not remain steady and you will lose your sense of judgement. You will want to stay away from that stinking thing because it is the cause of your anguish. You would like to go where there is something fragrant, because that augments your gaiety and cheerfulness. Before meditating if you burn some incense, you naturally feel mentally refreshed.

Living beings are affected by anguish. As far as the different kinds of anguish are concerned, there are four kinds of actions that human beings perform. Out of ignorance or attraction for physicality, man performs many actions which give pain and suffering while performing them, and leave pain and suffering after the performance. Suppose there is a rasagula [delicious sweet] competition among some men, and someone devours five kilograms of them. While eating, the person suffers in the sense that he is being coerced to eat because of the competition, that he is eating against his wish, only to emerge as a hero. You also know the painful consequences of eating a large quantity of sweets! Such an action brings pain while doing it, and pain after having done it.

The second type of action brings pain then pleasure. Suppose your friends have taken to devious ways of amassing wealth by accepting bribes, and you continue to live a hard but honest life full of poverty and trouble. You are, of course, suffering, but the consequences of your suffering will be rewarded in the sense that you will live with honor and respect. In this second type of action there was pain in the beginning, but the consequences will be happy.

The third type of action brings pleasure then

pain. In the third type of action there is a lot of pleasure in doing the action, but the effects of the action are very bad. Consider four people: Mr. A, Mr. B, Mr. C and Mr. D, traveling from Nagpur to Bombay. Mr. A, Mr. B, and Mr. C are traveling without tickets in the 1st class, air-conditioned coach. Mr. D, however, has a 3rd class ticket and is traveling in the crowded 3rd class compartment where he faces a lot of hardships. Mr. A, Mr. B, and Mr. C are in comfort and merriment. In the course of ticket-checking, Mr. A, Mr. B, and Mr. C are taken into police custody and Mr. D happily reaches his destination. The action of Mr. D brought pain then pleasure, whereas the actions of the others brought pleasure then pain. Remember that God is beyond the realm of the above-mentioned three actions.

The fourth type of action brings pleasure. Here there is pain neither in the performance of the action nor in the consequences of the action. This type of action is of God, and is also possible of man. What God does brings pleasure. And for men, spiritual *sádhana* brings pleasure. Yes, in the spiritual realm, man and God come to the same level or common point. The greater your *sádhana*, the closer you will be to God.

When action is performed both at the physical level and at the psychic level, it is called *karma*. God does not do anything at the physical level. For God everything is internal. For Him there is no external world. Everything is His internal psychic projection, nothing is external. For human beings there is internal psychic projection and external psychic projection. The man who projects a ghost in his mind and thinks about it continually, will project his mind externally and see the ghost in the external world. He who is not thinking about the ghost will not see it even at night. So for man there is an "internal" and an "external". If the thoughts of the ghost become dominant in the mind and if the remaining portion of the subconscious mind is suspended in or merged into that internal psychic projection, then the personality is lost. If the mind at that moment thinks that it has become a ghost, the person will act as if he were a ghost. This is a disease associated with hysteria. And people erroneously say that a ghost has entered the body! All this is psychological.

You perform actions by your mind and by your hands and legs. Sometimes you can do mental action but you cannot do physical action, because of fear of society and otherwise. The person who has narrowed the difference between his internal and external actions is a true man. The inner man and outer man should be one. If a dual personality develops side by side, and if the difference between the two personalities becomes very great, then the man dies. This double personality is very dangerous for human development. Make them one!

The wise will consider whether modern civilization is a true civilization or not. I am not an intellectual. But I know that the greatest defect of this civilization is that in it a double personality is developing. The gap between the internal man and external man is continually increasing. The gap is less, even now, in the illiterate, village folks.

However, in *Paramapuruśa* there is no scope for the existence of a dual personality. In God everything is internal; nothing is external. Everything is within, nothing is without. So this is the difference between the actions of a human being and of God, the created and the Creator.

When a man does any action, there is a reaction. Where there is action, there is equal and opposite reaction, provided the time, space and person remain unchanged. If one of the three factors changes, then the reaction will not be equal and opposite. The reaction will be a little greater or a little less. Suppose some evening at 7 P.M. Mr. X borrows 20,000 rupees from Mr. Y. If the money is not returned at the same instant it will have to be given back with some interest. You will have to pay back an amount greater than you took.

Reaction does not take place right then and there after an action. Reaction can take place after some time -- after a few hours or a few days, a few months, a few years or even a few decades. If you do a bad deed, you will have to bear the consequences of that deed, and you will have to pay interest on the action. Hence the reaction that you will have to bear will be greater than the action. Reaction is not in God, only in man. It has been said that God does not perform action in the external world, but man performs action. If man performs an inappropriate action in his mind, the mind will have to experience the reaction. Although it is said in the *shástras* [scriptures] that in *Káli Yuga* [this present dark age], mental sin is no sin, this actually means that mental sin is not punishable but should be avoided, and external sin is punishable and should undoubtedly be avoided.

If someone commits a theft, he will have to face punishment as a reaction. Theft is punishable and must be avoided. Someone who commits a theft in his mind does not harm any person of the world, and so his sin is not punishable. Of course, it should be avoided, because if the mind continually thinks, "I will steal, I will steal," then the man will commit the theft physically.

Benevolent action has a benevolent reaction; bad action has a bad reaction. A good action binds like a golden chain; a bad action binds like an iron chain. God does not suffer any reaction because there is nothing external to God. Everything is in Him and everything is Him. Whatever God does is within Himself and it is neither good nor bad. Your slapping a gentleman would be a wrong action, but slapping yourself would not be objectionable. No one will say anything to you. No one will file a defamation case against you, for whatever you have done is with yourself. So whatever God does is with Himself, and hence there is no reaction. This is the difference between man and God.

Every created thing, every living being needs a shelter. For example, Nagpur city is in the shelter of some district. The district is in the shelter of some state, and the state in some nation, nation in some continent, and so on. Even the sustenance of this earth is in the solar system, where the sun is the nucleus. The solar system has its home in the galaxy, in the cosmos. And what is the nucleus of the cosmos? The *Paramapuruśa*! But *Paramapuruśa* has no shelter. He does not depend on anything. On the other hand, man has to depend on something, on some shelter, on some recourse. If man wants to save himself from anguish, he will have to imbibe and adopt the qualities of God. Remember, the action bringing pleasure is common to both man and God. Hence man must encourage this type of action and this implies that he must do as much *sádhana* as possible. Even worldly activities must be performed as if they were a part of *sádhana*. Ascribe Godhood to every action that you do. Then you will be saved from anguish. Before doing something, you must make use of your *Guru mantra* [a practice ascribing Godhood to all worldly actions]. Every action then becomes a part of *sádhana*; it ceases to bind. There is no reaction if you perform every action by considering everyone your Self. Practice *madhuvidyá* [the sweet ideation that the Supreme is everywhere]!

Regarding shelter, a man must not think in terms of village, town, district. Only God must be his shelter, and he must think that he is in the shelter of God alone. Only His shelter, only His boat can take us across the stream of life.

By taking His refuge, man will become God. And you must take His refuge now; it will be difficult later.

God is indescribable, undefinable. He is the very embodiment of love. As far as worldly connections and relationships are concerned, all things are mutual, nothing is unilateral. You pay a shopkeeper some money, and he gives you the thing you want. The relationship is

YOU ARE NEVER ALONE

OR HELPLESS.

THE FORCE THAT

GUIDES THE STARS,

GUIDES YOU TOO.

mutual. You cannot get anything from the shopkeeper if you do not pay him for it. Also you do not pay the shopkeeper money without taking something in return. Your relationship is mutual. This is business. When the connection is unilateral, when you give without taking anything in return, it is *seva* [service]. The businessman advertises that he has been "serving the society for the last twenty years." Actually he has been doing no service, he has been doing business. He takes money to supply some commodity in return. Similarly, man performs worldly actions like eating, speaking, etc. for his pleasure. Whatever man does for the happiness and satisfaction of God is called *prema* [love]. Love is unilateral; all worldly work is mutual.

God does not do anything for Himself. God is love personified, because what He does is for the service of living beings. He is the abode of love. His love is ineffable. He is inexplicable. Man is goaded by his selfishness and guided by his limited intellect in the affairs of the world. I remember hearing somewhere, that a gentleman was asked to laugh. He, being a businessman, retorted, "What profit will I get by my laughing?" Before doing something, man sees whether it would be profitable for him to do that thing. This is not the case with God. He belongs to all. He is for all.

While God is inexplicable, we can say something about the nature of man. For instance, we say that this person is eccentric; this gentleman is pure of heart; this man is good but for his vitriolic temper; and so on. In a word, man is explicable but God is inexplicable. *Vyása*, a poet of Ancient India, wrote the *Puránas* [ancient scriptures] for public education and for praising God's divine characteristics, so he elaborated on God. But this should not have been done because God is inexplicable, He is indescribable. God cannot be brought within the scope of language; He is beyond it. He cannot be spoken of; He is even beyond the mind. So it is not possible for the scriptures to write about Him. And you know, *Vyása* after having written the scripture, apologized to God and beseeched to be forgiven in these words:

"You are beyond form, and yet I have described you. This is my first fault and crime. You are beyond all qualities, yet I have described your qualities like compassion, mercy, etc. This is my second fault and crime. You are omnipresent, yet I have stressed and propagated the importance of pilgrimages. By saying that pilgrimages to a place, or a dip in some holy river would be something virtuous and capable of producing certain material benefits, I have affronted you and your omniscience. This is my third crime. O God, I have consciously committed these three crimes. Forgive me, O Lord!"

Yes, God is infinite. Man can be described: Tom is of this kind, Dick of that kind. Man must contemplate God. Then he too will become inexplicable; he too will become an embodiment of love.

You work with one brain, but God works with millions and millions of brains. You consider yourself erudite after reading a few books and say, "Where is God? Show me." Ah! Do you have the eye to see Him? If a blind man is asked to see an elephant, what will he see? To see the elephant you need eyes. Man has two eyes, both in the front. One eye at the back and one eye in the front might have served the purpose. The two eyes are in the front, and man cannot even see what is happening behind him. But God "sees" with an infinite number of eyes. He sees even what you do clandestinely. He "sees" what you are thinking in your mind. You [pointing to a *sádhaka* from Hyderabad] think that it would have been convenient for you if Nagpur had been closer to Hyderabad, but for God there is no such thing as distance. He does not have to go anywhere. His one foot is here in the tent and His other foot may be in your house in Hyderabad. You must remember that in the case of absolute cognition there is absolute speed or absolute pause, but in the realm of relativity, there can never be absolute speed or absolute pause; everywhere there is relative speed and relative pause.

He is in this world of five fundamental factors. And in this psychic world, in the spheres of the mind, He exists in His all-pervasiveness. He has created every sphere of the mind, and He exists everywhere.

But the limited being is in a limited region of this crude world. If someone says that he is an M.A. in

Geography, and if I ask him the number of houses in Nagpur or the number of bricks in the houses, he will not be able to reply. How many bricks are there in Nagpur is certainly a question of Geography, but I have not met any M.A. in Geography who could answer my question.

The inference is that human knowledge is imperfect and you can never claim to be perfect in any human knowledge. The pride of learning is therefore meaningless. Man has nothing of which he can be proud. If at all he has anything of which he can be proud, it is God. You can certainly be proud of your Father who is perfect and divine. "I am the son of God"; this is the right type of pride. Other than this there is nothing of which you can be proud.

Man knows only a few things of the recent past. He does not even know what will happen the next moment. But God knows everything. He is omniscient, because the world of relativity lies within Him. He is the knower of the past and the future. Man's knowledge is quite limited. If those who have passed their M.A.'s are asked to appear in an examination right now, I think that not one would pass. Even if the same questions that you attempted in your earlier examination are again given to you now, you would not succeed, because you would have forgotten quite a lot of what you learned before.

Men are guided by superiority complexes or by inferiority complexes. Suppose someone passes his M.A., and the people in his village are all illiterate. When he goes to his village he will have such an air of pride that he will not spontaneously mix with the people and freely talk with them. He might also have the inferiority of belonging to a backward village when he is among city-dwellers. In man the feelings of big and small crop up. Man does not have a dispassionate outlook.

Conversely, God looks at the stupid and the wise, the black and the white, the tall and the short, and at everyone -- with the same eye. Man, however, thinks about big and small. He flatters the big and disdains or neglects the small. For God there is no differentiation. God is for everyone. At the time of sorrow, you say, "O God, save me," and the wicked man says, "O God, save me." God listens even to the wicked, but you despise the wicked. I once said that God cannot do two things: He cannot create another God like Himself, though He can create everything else, and He cannot hate anyone. Even if God desires to hate someone, He cannot do so. Those who are in heaven and those who burn in the fire of hell are both equally dear to God. God is compassionate to everyone. No one is without His support. If a mean creature in hell weeps and says, "O God, now I can no longer bear the torture. Save me," then God will listen to him and protect him as He would protect anyone else. But you do not have this characteristic. When you see a wicked person in pain, you say, "Ah! it serves him right!" You have intense hatred for that wicked man.

You can be dictated to by others, but God cannot be dictated to by anyone. This is the fundamental difference between you and God. In spite of this, God has blessed you with a wondrous thing -- your mind. The nature of this thing, this mind, is that as it thinks so it becomes. So what can you do very conveniently? Merge your mind in God. Taking the ideation of God, you will become God yourself, and all the qualities and characteristics of God will come in you. God cannot be two. You will merge with God and become that one God. You will be established in blessedness for eternity!

○

> *The persons who can dedicate their all to the thought of the Great and the inspiration of the Supreme are verily the greatest heroes. Such heroes indeed are the virtuous and they alone are capable of taking human history from darkness to light.*

THE TRUE DEVOTEE

The demarcation between right and wrong, sin and piety, "do's and don'ts," exists only for those who are not true devotees. True devotees can think only of *Paramapuruśa*; their every action is to please *Paramapuruśa*. For them, there is only *sádhana* and selfless service to the universe; and because selfless service is to please the Lord, that also helps *sádhana*. *Tapah* [selfless service] is part of *sádhana*. True devotees are unable to think of right and wrong; because they wish only to please *Paramapuruśa* they can only do good, and all their actions will be benevolent. So you are not just to worry about right and wrong, about "do's and don'ts" -- you are to develop that true devotion for *Paramapuruśa*.

There is a story about Lord *Krśńa*, that He became very ill and a great number of devotees came to cure Him, but all with no success. The followers of Lord *Krśńa* became agitated and prayed to Him to direct them how to cure Him. Whereupon Lord *Krśńa*

declared, "When My true devotee comes to Me with the dust from his feet, and when I touch that dust, that will be My cure." The followers were taken aback -- they could not think to do such a thing -- to have Lord *Krśńa* touch their dirty feet! Yet when a simple peasant boy heard of this he came forward with the reply, "I do not know if I am a true devotee of Lord *Krśńa*, but I do love Lord *Krśńa* and if the dust of my feet will cure Him, I am most glad to oblige Him."

Such is the true devotee, and such devotion you are all to develop, through your *sádhana* and your service. But of course, until you develop such devotion, you must distinguish what to do from what not to do! ○

THE OCEAN OF GRACE

From the inanimate to the animate goes the process of evolution. Consider a piece of stone for instance. It has neither the power of action nor the sensation of mind. What is the reason? It is because hitherto there has been no manifestation of mind in the stone at all. Consider the trees and plants that are more animate than the stone. There is activity in them. They grow, draw the vital juice from the earth, maintain their species by creating seeds in their own bodies and enjoy and suffer pleasure and pain when taken care of or hurt. We see in them the manifestation of consciousness or animation, for mind has awakened in them. Thus progressing on the path of mental development, we see in man its greatest manifestation. Just as evolution takes place from the subtle to the crude, similarly the unit entity reverts step by step from the crude to the subtle, towards the same Absolute Consciousness from whence it came. It is just like the waves of the sea rippling back from whence they have come.

Now, just how much should a man strive on his

return journey? He has to be alert, so that he may easily end the journey in his characteristic Self, without being distracted by the impact of his petty selfishness. Then alone shall we call him self-purified. Then alone shall he become saturated with God, within and without.

To become self-purified one has to make some effort -- this effort is known as *sádhana*. The greatest *sádhana* is that which comprises devotion, action and knowledge. The middling *sádhana* is that which comprises devotion and action; and the lowest *sádhana* is that which comprises only tall talks. Knowledge cannot exist without action and devotion -- that which does exist is the junk or garbage of knowledge! The ability of a *sádhaka* is not assessed on the basis of his common or worldly knowledge. It is assessed on the basis of firmness or steadiness of his knowledge, devotion and action. By steadiness I mean unflinching intensity of zeal and earnestness. Just by saying that candy is sweet, one does not receive the taste of that candy. One has to make some efforts to obtain it and eat it.

A mouthful of tall talks alone cannot achieve *Brahma*. An almanac forecasts that there will be so much rain this year. But mere knowledge of such forecasts does not save the crops of a farmer. No amount of squeezing the almanac will produce even a drop of water. One has to do *sádhana* to habituate one's mind in a God-ward direction in order to attain Him.

If a man without intuition studies the scriptures a million times, or lectures on God, his God will ever remain the bookish God and not the clairvoyant, clairaudient and apprehensible God. Just as one seeing in water the reflection of a fruit dangling overhead from the branch of a tree cannot taste the fruit, similarly an erudite scholar, versed in the philosophies, will remain far away from God if he refrains from God-*sádhana*. No matter how vastly learned you become in worldly lore, you can know nothing about God, for along with your knowledge, a vanity of learning also grows in you. As a result you go on enhancing the volume of your burden unnecessarily by giving importance to your small ego. This burden becomes the cause of your sufferings and enjoyments, not your salvation.

You will come across many such people who do not meditate themselves, but will run after great spiritual men in order to hear their sermons. These people are totally in the wrong. Only running after great men will be to no avail. A man has to establish himself in the path of realization of God by doing *sádhana* himself. God does not bestow His mercy upon anybody after seeing how great a speaker he is or how many books he has read. Only the one who has devotion extracts His mercy.

God can be realized even through having a wee bit of God's Grace. Consider a very intelligent boy for instance. If his teacher does not teach him how to read and write, he will not be able to be a learned man, in spite of his having the potential to become one. Similarly, all men have the ability or potentiality of spiritual development, of establishing themselves in God, but for lack of a worthy guide it cannot take a practical shape. That is why a spiritual preceptor or *Sadguru* is necessary -- His Grace is indispensable. His Grace is but God's Grace, for God is the Ocean of Grace. ○

> *What is the meaning of* sádhú [*saint*]? *Really* sádhú *means those in whose contact others become good. One is not a* sádhú *simply by wearing saffron dress. Those who have the capability of attracting others alone are* sádhús. *One can be a* sádhú *even in a suit.*

SERVICE

At the time of rendering service, a man's feeling should be that the object of his service is God. Then there will be no room for conceit. Conceit is the cause of the fall of man. Therefore, for overcoming conceit, we shall have to regard the object of our service as God.

When you render service to anyone, you must mentally address Him with sincere devotion, "O Lord, O God! Oblige me by accepting my services. You are merciful to me, and for this reason You have appeared before me as a living being to offer me this very precious opportunity of rendering services to You." By maintaining such sentiments, conceit will not arise in you, nor will the reactions of your actions bind you. The principal cause for the bondage of the fruits of action is conceit or yearning for fame. Suppose a certain man donates a sum of 1,000 rupees to a particular institution. The next day he looks anxiously for his name in the newspaper. If his name does not appear in the paper, with an air of conceit he brags amongst his relatives, "I donated a thousand rupees, but I do not desire to earn fame and therefore I have not published my name in the paper." The desire for fame is hidden in that man's mind. Surely, he did not make the donation with the spirit of service. But when you perform actions by transplanting the idea of God on the person served, there will be no possibility of any arrogance or any idea of earning fame growing in your mind. Then you will realize that through the grace of God you have the opportunity of serving God. Our hands and feet are not ours, they are His, and by serving Himself with those hands and feet He sports with Himself.

Such an action alone is an action without attachment. Through this alone can man attain salvation from the bondage of *karma*. You must feel that the person served is *Brahma*, His finite manifestation. Never, even by mistake, take the object of your service to be a man, or a living being. By working with these feelings of *Brahma*, gradually you will be able to perceive *Brahma* in everything.

It should be borne in mind that the reaction of an action is intimately involved with the action itself. You are free to act but you are bound to undergo its reaction. The moment you do an act, the seed for its reaction is simultaneously being sown, and its consequence has to be undergone. There is no escape from it.

It is only by adopting a special sentiment that

you will not be attached to *karma*, because the arrogance of your "I-feeling" will not have an opportunity to arise. This sentiment is that by the Lord's directions you are serving Him. If you surrender the subjective feeling of your actions to the Lord, then the reactions will also belong to Him.

One must see here how the consequences of actions are annihilated through service. Where there is arrogance of "I-feeling", there the consequences exist with the actions, begetting corresponding consequences. Where the "I" is the doer, there the same "I" is the receiver of the consequences. In detached actions, the "I" is not the doer, and as such it is not liable to reap the consequences . In an unattached action there is no bondage of the consequences, because whatever the doer does is consigned to *Brahma*, and therefore the consequences of the actions are also consigned to *Brahma*.

There are many persons who have energy but do not work. They are lethargic. But there are also persons who work hard even if they do not have energy. They are persons who die working. This is very good. But better would be to work even while dying.

Regard yourself as an instrument of God and go on doing your work in a detached manner. Here a question may arise whether a person suffering from pain is only reaping the consequences of his actions, and in these circumstances, would it be proper to serve him? The answer is very simple. I will not even think that he is reaping the consequences of his actions. I will, at that time, have to think that in pursuit of a particular plan, God Himself is suffering distress and in this way, He is affording me an opportunity to render services. Out of His grace He is obliging me by accepting my services. Inscrutable are the designs of God. Look upon the distressed with a divine sentiment.

But while taking this sentiment, one has to make sure that the sentiment is born out of love and not out of fear. Fear does not generate love. There will be no service in absence of love, and all your service will become meaningless. What is love? Love must be selfless. You rear hens, you love those hens, you feed them with paddy. If anyone takes your hens, you become angry and come to blows with him. But is this selfless love? You are feeding the hens for your benefit. There you are motivated by the sentiment that one day this hen will lay eggs and you will earn money by selling them.

Love has to be untarnished. Entertain divine feelings by saturating love wherever you have to perform service. It is meaningless to love out of fear. Where there is no love, there cannot be complete surrender of self, and service also will be fruitless there.

The life of a person becomes mechanical if he remains overwhelmed with the sentiment that one must do such acts, one must perform such service, one must rise in this manner and sit in this manner, and get up in this manner, and so on. Happiness disappears there. For this reason, such ritualism cannot be called real *karma*. To serve others at one's sacrifice is called penance. In the absence of love, service rendered and penance undergone for show only are fruitless. All ritualistic devotion, sham penance, counting of beads, etc., are meant only for public show. True love and the Supreme Goal are lost sight of. *Brahma* cannot be attained through any show actions, because in ritualistic thoughts, the sweetness of happiness is lacking. Divine Bliss is easily available only to those who base their *sádhana* on love.

Let everyone render services to the world in accordance with his capacity. Work for the welfare of the living beings to the best of your ability. If a poor man thinks that he cannot render economic service since he has no money, he is wrong. The poor man's charity of a few pennies has identical value with the millionaire's charity of thousands: rather the charity of those few pennies outweighs the thousands.

As long as you exist, you have to perform service. The moment you stop, you will fall in an abyss.

You should not do this. It is your *dharma* [nature] to carry yourself from narrowness to vastness, from greatness to divinity. It is against your nature to allow yourself to fall into an abyss. You long for eternal bliss, you endeavor for eternal life, and you are fused with that very unending life in the circulation of your blood and in the rhythmic vibrations of the contractions of your heart. You have been listening day and night to the voice of eternal youth. In the state of Supreme Attainment and Supreme Realization, you will be infused with boundless knowledge. O man! be established in the radiance of godliness, in manliness, because yours is a path of revolution. Yours is not a path of extra caution and hesitant movement. You are travelers of a difficult path. You have to march ahead, with head held high and with your chest forward. You have not a moment to stagger or look behind. ○

SHELTER TO THE SINNERS ALSO

Now this Supreme *Puruṡa* is the Father of the blessed, of the virtuous. He is their supreme shelter. But is He not the Father of those who are not virtuous, those who are sinners? Certainly He is their Father. He is the Father of the sinners also. Otherwise where are the sinners to go? He must give shelter to the sinners also. He knows the past of all His daughters and all His sons. Even then He loves them, doesn't He? Suppose the Supreme Father says that He is the Father of the virtuous only, not the Father of the sinners; is He justified in this? Has He the right to say this? Then the sinners will challenge His authority. They will say, "No, Supreme Father, you have no right to say that you are not the Father of sinners." When He is the Father of the universe, then do sinners live beyond the scope of the universe? No. Then the sinners may say," O Father, if you are not the Supreme, if you are not our Father, then please expel us to some place outside the universe." The Supreme Father is the Lord of the entire universe. He is the Witness of all the witnesses. He is the King of all kings.

People may think, "Will God be kind to us? Will He not be angry, since our past is full of ills and depravities?" To Him sinners or the virtuous make no difference: On the contrary, vanity may be found in a virtuous man. He may think, "I have done no wrong." But a sinner is a helpless man. He has nothing to his credit. He is absolutely shelterless. So God first extends His arms to the sinners. Giving help and shelter to the helpless and the shelterless is indeed real greatness. If God fails to give shelter to the sinners, we may infer that hatred abides even in God and that He distinguishes between a sinner and a virtuous man. What does a mother do? Of her two sons, if one is strong and the other weak, she takes more care of the weak child. Similarly, God showers His blessings more upon the helpless.

"Even if a sinner ideates on Me, if he accepts Me as his only object of ideation," says the Lord, "he will be free from all worldly fetters, from all worldly bondages." He must attain salvation. He must be freed from all sins, from all bondages of sins by the Supreme Father. So for the virtuous and also for the sinners, the Supreme Father is the only shelter; the Supreme Father is the only object of ideation. What are the sinners to do? They are to forget their past, and they are to move ahead on the path of spirituality to attain that Supreme Stance, to come in direct contact with the Supreme Father.

Your future is assured, your problems are to be solved by the Supreme Father. You are to serve the universe as the ideal daughters and sons of the Supreme Father. You need not be anxious, you must not have any worries or anxieties for your personal problems. Your problems are to be solved by the Supreme Father. As the ideal daughters and ideal sons of the Supreme Father, serve the children of that Father.

Go forward. Forget all about your past. Advancement and progress must come your way. Victory shall be yours. ○

It is action that makes a man great. Be great by your sádhana, by your service and by your sacrifice.

THE LORD'S PALMS

The palms of the Lord are everywhere. Whatever is offered to Him, good or bad, He receives; and whenever and wherever it is offered to Him, He receives it. The scriptures say that ordinary human beings of the world use their powers of discrimination before they decide upon what to receive and what not to receive. They accept only that which they like, and reject that which they do not like. On the other hand, the elevated souls do not accept anything from anyone. But *Paramapuruśa* is entirely different from these two groups. He makes no discrimination whatsoever, and accepts all that is offered to Him by any of His children. People normally offer sentient things to different deities: white flowers are generally offered to them. But to *Paramapuruśa* one may even offer red flowers, which are a flow of *rajoguńa* [mutative] color. This is because *Paramapuruśa* has His palms ready to receive anything and everything. One may offer his reverence or his abuse: the Lord's palms are ever extended to receive it.

Once the Lord *Buddha* was camping in a mango orchard. A large number of people were always accepting the path shown by the Lord *Buddha*, but a particular individual and his group were much opposed to Lord *Buddha*. It so happened that his group, without him, came to the mango orchard where Lord *Buddha* was camping and was influenced by the Lord *Buddha*, and accepted Buddhism. This news greatly agitated this man, and he came in anger to the orchard and started abusing Lord *Buddha* in all sorts of ways. Lord *Buddha* maintained His usual equipoise through all this. A man feels happy and encouraged in abusing someone only if he finds that the person is affected by his acts of abuse. This man found Lord *Buddha* undisturbed and was greatly disappointed, finding all his hard labor gone to waste. When he had been abusing Lord *Buddha* for quite some time and his stock of bad words was coming to an end, the Lord *Buddha* urged him to listen to Him. Lord *Buddha* asked the man, "Suppose you give something to somebody and he accepts it; then the ownership of the thing is transferred to the receiver, isn't it?" The man agreed. The Lord *Buddha* continued, "And if the man rejects the offering, will the thing not be returned to the owner?" The man again agreed. Lord *Buddha* concluded, "All the words given by you have not been accepted by me!"

But *Paramapuruśa* has His palms ever ready to accept all that is offered by His children anywhere in the world. The palms of human beings are so small -- they can receive and contain so little. Their palms simply cannot receive more than this. But the palms of *Paramapuruśa* are large enough to receive any quantity from all His children at the same time. ○

THE DIVINE WILL

Where mind is operative in a structure, that structure is controlled by the mind; but structures in which mind is not expressed are controlled and operated by the mind of the Supreme Being. A man, for instance, moves from this place to that place by his mind; but the wind blows, and water flows according to the dictates of the Cosmic Mind. The movements controlled by the Supreme Being are all from inanimate to animate, and from crude to subtle. In other words, they are movements towards God. We may say that the Supreme Being is drawing everything unto Himself.

Human beings are moved and guided by their own unit minds, but even here where matters of collective importance are concerned, they are not absolutely free -- there the Macrocosm asserts Its mind.

When a man moves in a line opposite the pull of the Supreme Being, this is movement towards degradation. Movement is a must, whether it is towards progress or degradation -- whether towards hell or superman. Those animals and inanimate objects whose minds are not developed have no chance of being degraded since they have no choice of movement except in the direction of the Supreme. But man has the freedom of choice between progress and degradation.

If only the movement according to the will of the Supreme Being is movement towards progress, the question arises how to ascertain the desire of God. Man's small mind, enclosed in a box of bones, is incapable of knowing the secrets of the Cosmic Mind. It is difficult to know the unexpressed desire of the Supreme Self. But wherever there is difficulty, the solution lies nearby. Every disease has a curative herb near the source of the disease itself.

Suppose you have to ascertain what Mr. X would like to eat -- rasagulas or gulabjamun [two types of Indian sweets]. How would you know this? Being a gentleman he will not express his desire. And God is also a gentleman -- His desires are not all on the surface. A villager may blurt out his desires, but a refined man will not -- and God is refined.

But there is one way out. Start loving Mr. X and your minds will meet and you will know his desires. This is the path followed by the devotees. They love God and know His mind; they tune their minds in the same wave-length and direction.

The difference between a *sádhaka* and a philosopher is this: the *sádhaka* learns philosophy for the sake of convincing others, not for himself. He is content to love God.

Imagine a devotee and a philosopher being in a mango grove. The philosopher will start counting the trees, their branches, and the mangoes in the orchard. While he is thus wasting his time, the devotee is enjoying the sweet juice of the mangoes. The devotee says, "God is mine -- I shall love Him and understand His will and act accordingly."

Those who do not love God are also not completely free to act. They have to follow the Divine Will perforce. Some follow Him out of love, others out of fear. There is some element of fear in love also. My slightest mistake may pain the person I love, and hence this fear keeps me straight on the path of love. Man alone has the chance to follow God with love; other beings have to do so compulsorily.

Those who are afraid of God are not *sádhakas*. All want to avoid fear. God is fear to fear. All are afraid of the terrible -- and God is a terror to the terrible. Thus being our enemy's enemy, God is our best friend.

Movement is life. God is the movement of the innermost vital energy [*práña*]. If God removes himself, one will no longer exist.

> *Even if a boy says something logical, it should be accepted; and even if the lotus-born* Brahma [*the mythological creator of the universe*] *says something illogical it should be rejected like a straw.*

God is one who purifies the purification. He is the Purity of the pure. People consider a dip in the Ganges as a purifying act. If this were true, the fish and animals who live in the Ganges would be the purest of beings, since they live 24 hours a day in the Ganges!

God lives in every heart, and He is the Purifier of purity. So all that you have to do to be pure is to search your heart, contact the Supreme Being there and be pure. Why need you go outside for purification??

Power corrupts and absolute power corrupts absolutely. Power without devotion is a force leading to degradation. You should not forget that God is the source of all ultimate power. He can snatch your power from you in a minute. This body of yours wherein you are a tenant belongs to the Supreme Law. He can evict you in a moment, without prior notice. ○

JIÑÁNA, KARMA & BHAKTI
KNOWLEDGE, ACTION & DEVOTION

One is to attain Him, to come in contact with the Divine Father, by *jiñána, karma* and *bhakti*. What is *jiñána? Jiñána* is spiritual knowledge, not mundane knowledge. Mundane knowledge is distorted knowledge. It is not knowledge at all. Spiritual knowledge is the knowledge. But what is spiritual knowledge? One must know what one is, what is one's goal. This is the spiritual knowledge.

Then comes *karma. Karma* means action. If one knows what one is, what is one's desideratum, then one will have to move toward the terminus of his life. This movement, this practical approach, this actional approach is called *karma*. And after *karma*, when one comes near Him, one is to be united or unified with Him. This process of unification is devotion, *bhakti.*

Bhakti Yoga can be divided into two broad categories: one is attributional devotion and another is non-attributional devotion. In attributional devotion, there are three stages. The first is static devotion. In static devotion the devotee says, "Oh my Lord, I am your devotee. Mr. X is my enemy. Please destroy him." In the case of static devotion, the devotee doesn't want to be with the Lord, the devotee wants something bad or harsh to be done to his enemy. That is the devotion of the worst type. As it was not his longing to become one with the Father, so he will never be united with the Father. Also, the Supreme Father is the Supreme Father of that enemy also, so He may or may not kill his enemy. Static devotion is no devotion.

Then comes mutative devotion. In this case the devotee says to the Lord, "I am your devotee. Please give me money. Please give me name and fame." The boy wants only toys from the mother. If the boy starts crying, the mother must leave her duties and attend to the child. But if the child just wants the toys, he will never get the mother. Here also the *sádhaka* didn't express the desire to become one with the Father, so he won't attain salvation. He won't become a devotee. *Yogi* means one who finally is unified with the Supreme Self. Also this type of devotee asked for worldly property. You know, worldly properties are limited. The number of dollars may be great, but it is not infinite. So the Lord may or may not fulfill your desire. He has to look after the interests of so many children. He has so many children, He can't fulfill your unjustified demand. So this mutative devotion is not devotion at all.

Now there comes the third type of attributional

devotion, sentient devotion. In this case the devotee says, "I am your devotee. But Oh Lord, I am an old man. Give me something concrete. I want salvation. And you know I am disgusted with the world. My digestive organs have become disordered. I can't eat anything. Please give me peace. Please give me peace." This is sentient devotion because here the aspirant, the devotee, doesn't want anything physical. So it is better than static and mutative devotion because he wants salvation from the Supreme Father, but he doesn't want the Supreme Father. So he is not a *Yogi*. A *Yogi* has to unify himself with the Father. A *Yogi* will not demand any toys from the Father.

Then there comes the non-attributional devotion. In non-attributional devotion there are two phases. One is called *rágánugá bhakti*, another is called *rágátmiká*. In *rágánugá* devotion, the devotee says, "Oh my Lord, I love you because in loving You I get pleasure. I want nothing from You. I want to love You because I get pleasure." This is non-attributional devotion, but it is not the highest form of devotion.

The highest form of devotion is called *rágátmiká*. In *rágátmiká* the devotee says, "Oh Lord I love You. I want to love You. And why do I want to love You? Because I want that my love should give You pleasure. I don't want any pleasure. I love You not to get pleasure but to give You pleasure." This is the highest

> *Knowing oneself is the real knowledge, serving all with the ideation of God is the real action, and the vow to please God the real devotion.*

form of devotion. And by dint of this type of devotion, *rágátmiká* devotion, the *Yogi* comes in closest contact with the Supreme Self and becomes one with Him. When his love is to give pleasure to the Lord and not to enjoy pleasure for himself, his mind gets subjectivated. That is, his mind gets metamorphosed into the mind of the Lord, and that's why this *rágátmiká bhakti* devotion is the only devotion. By this devotion, the *Yogi* gets established into this stance of Supreme Beatitude. The man and his God become One. This is the only goal of human life -- to become One with Him.

When one comes near the Supreme Father, he has to address the Father, "Oh Father, give me shelter on your blissful lap, on your graceful lap." To say this, one has to establish a relationship of implicit faith and sincerest love with the Father. This implicit faith blended with spiritual zeal is called devotion. So knowledge and action will help you in developing devotion, but your unification with the Supreme Self will be established with the help of devotion only. Where there is action, and where there is knowledge, but there is a lack of devotion, nothing can be done. In the life of a spiritual aspirant, in the life of a *Yogi*, nothing can be done if there is lack of devotion. So you daughters, you sons, you must remember that you will have to develop devotion, implicit devotion blended with spiritual zeal. And that devotion will help you. Devotion is the only faculty to help you, to establish you in the Supreme Beatitude.○

LIVE ACCORDING TO GOD'S DESIRE

You have just said, "Victory unto Bábá! [Bábá ki jai!]" -- but I say, "Victory unto you." As a human being, as a spiritualist, as a spiritual missionary, when you will be victorious, you will be happy. But happier will I be, many times more.

Whatever object or idea there is in this relative world, there is a reason behind each and every one. The reason may be known to you, or may not be known to you. But there is a reason. When you get quite tired of worldly activities and sit in a lonely place, you think, "Why have I come into this world?" You might not know the reason, but He, the one who has manifested His *lülá* [play] everywhere, knows the reason. You might consider yourself inferior, but you are not so to Him.

Take, for example, your body, your mind, and the innumerable tiny cells of your body. Each cell gives rise to a particular thought. Such specialities there are in the human structure! The Creator has created this body carefully, with the utmost care; He even knows where a particular spot in your nerve is. You are not small. A doll may consider itself small, and it may be considered small by some, but the Creator of the doll would never consider His creation valueless.

All that comes within the scope of relativity has a reason behind its existence. Even the existence of an eighty-year-old man and woman has a reason behind it. *Paramapuruśa* has kept you in the world; there is definitely a reason behind it. Never let inferiority arise in you. You are the children of *Paramapuruśa* -- how can you be inferior? If someone says that you are low, valueless, he is absolutely wrong. *Paramapuruśa*, your Creator, is a Great Entity. How can He create anything inferior?

Many say that Nature creates. But this is wrong. What can Nature create? The style, the system in which the Operative Principle [*Prakrti*] operates is known as Nature. There is a style of singing, of dancing; there is a style for doing each and every action. The style of the work of the Operative Principle is known as Nature. How can the style create? Only the One whose style it is can create. Nature can do nothing. The Operative Principle operates according to the desire of *Paramapuruśa*. If *Paramapuruśa* did not permit it, then the Operative Principle would be unable to create; even a blade of grass would not move. Right from *Brahma* to a blade of grass, it is all His desire. Forget the talk about

Nature. To talk of Nature is to talk of a philosophy of the time when man worshipped stones, trees, etc.

Without His desire nothing will happen. You might say in a meeting, "I challenge *Paramapuruśa.*" Having spoken the word "challenge," you might find that your raised fist remains raised and your voice is choked. Nothing can happen without His desire.

You have come according to His wish, by none else's. Leave everything to Him. An astrologer predicts your death on a particular day, and advises you to wear lockets to counteract the effects of stars and planets. But doesn't the astrologer himself die?

You will live according to His desire; you will die, too, according to His desire. I told you to take the name of the One only. Depend on One only, not on two. Death is not painful for you, because in death too you attain Him. Merge into Him with all your love.

He has given you your organs. Utilize them for Him. With your voice sing His name, His praise, His *kiirtans.* With your mind think of Him.

One who does not do this wastes his life. It is your duty to preach this message from door to door to all human beings. ○

OFFERING OF COLORS

The main object of your spring color festival [an Indian festival involving throwing of colored water] is not playing with external colors. It really means the offering to God of the colors of different objects which have dyed or stained your mind. When this practice of offering Him your own colors, your own fancies, becomes feasible and easy, you will then merge in Him. Your unit-ego will become one with the Cosmic Ego. The two will become a single entity. Whichever way you turn your eyes, you will see only Him in His ever-surging glory. There is neither "I" nor "you". By an everlasting mutual pact, the final curtain will have fallen, ending all clashes of "I" and "you". At that stage if you call God by "I" you are right in calling Him so; if you call Him by "He" you are equally right; if you call Him by "You", again you are right.

The amount of your attainment of Him will be proportionate to your self-surrender. Remember you have to offer your own entity -- not money, rice, bananas or other crude things. The give and take of crude things is a business transaction. If you want to attain God's bliss, offer your own soul. If you want to have the Great

"I", give away your own little "I".

You have to give the full sixteen annas [the full rupee]. Giving fifteen annas and holding back one anna will not do. Complete surrender is the way.

Remember, self-surrender does not mean suicide. On the contrary, your soul will have its full expression. Your entity will not get contracted, for contraction is inert, static. Hence in the *sádhana* of self-surrender, the ego gets expanded, not contracted.

In the *Mahábharata*, an Indian epic, a cruel courtier was pulling the dress of *Draopadii*, the virtuous heroine, and she was holding her garment tightly with one hand while invoking Lord *Krśńa* with the other -- "Come, O Lord, to my rescue!" But the Lord did not then come forward to save her from shame. When *Draopadii* found no means of escape, she then gave up her grip on the cloth and appealed to the Lord most piteously with both hands outstretched, "O Lord, I surrender my all to You. Do what You think fit and proper." The Lord immediately rescued her. That is why I say that you will have to dedicate yourselves to His Feet wholly and unreservedly. You will earn godliness in proportion to the extent that you surrender yourselves, and finally, after merging that acquired godliness of yours in His Entity, you will attain eternal bliss.

God bless you. ○

After millions of animal lives, created beings attain human forms. That is why all the shástras [scriptures] speak of the rarity of human life. The wise make proper utilization of all objects -- this utilization alone makes the existence of the object worthy. You have achieved human frame -- you must make it meaningful by your sádhana, service, and sacrifice. Engage yourself in such useful pursuits that even the worst of your enemies hardly has any chance to despise you; utilize yourself in such a manner so as to have satisfaction in your mind also, that you never wasted your time uselessly on this earth.

DAGDHABIIJA: BURNT SEED

Is misery less even if one is bound up with chains made of gold? No -- bondage is bondage, be it made of gold or iron. The bondage of good actions is of gold and of bad actions, iron. Either of them is to be broken off. One has to avoid bad actions so that the chains of iron might not be forged. Good actions are to be done, but the chains of gold are to be offered at the feet of *Paramapuruśa:* "I do not desire the fruits of my good actions, O Lord! I offer them to thee."

As long as the physical body exists some actions are bound to be performed. No one can help acting. Respiration itself is an action. One may not desire to do any action and so he sleeps -- yet to sleep, too, is an action. Actions have to be performed, not bad actions but good ones which are to be offered to Him.

Even after millions of eons, the reactions of the actions are not exhausted. How will the reactions of the actions be exhausted? When the reactions are undergone, then only are they exhausted.

One has performed good actions, and so their fruits are to be enjoyed; so it is with bad actions. Hence one must be cautious while performing actions. After that, repentance will reap no benefit.

There are so many stages of *sádhakas*. Some say "O *Paramapuruśa*, please get my reactions [*saḿskáras*] exhausted as soon as possible; whatever is there, give it to me." Others say, "I am ready to bear the fruits of my own actions, and I am also ready to bear the fruits of others' actions."

There are varieties of feelings. Some want to carry the burden of others so that others might not be in trouble. *Sádhakas* are at different stages and their feelings are just according to their stages. While doing *sádhana*, a *sádhaka* reaches a stage where 100% devotion [*púrna bhakti*, "full devotion"] is aroused for *Paramapuruśa*. Then he remains unassailed even if a cyclone of misery attacks him. He may feel maximum torture in his mind, but he cares little for it, taking it to be the benediction of *Paramapuruśa* Himself. The torture is there but he derives bliss in it. The *sádhaka* of that stage is called *dagdhabiija*.

Biija means seed; *dagdha* means burnt. Whenever a seed is sown it begets a plant. But when the seed is burnt, the plant is not produced. A *sádhaka* becomes *dagdhabiija* when he has no more pain and pleasure of his own. He who has surrendered completely and has not kept in his hand even a single penny of it, he alone is *dagdhabiija*.

All carry their own burdens, but if a *dagdhabiija sádhaka* so desires he can carry the burdens of others also. And those that want to carry the burdens of others do lessen the burden of *Paramapuruśa* indirectly. This you should remember.

Don't be concerned with your individual problems at all. Be prepared to carry your own burden and be prepared also to carry the burdens of others. Then alone are you brave. Be *dagdhabiija*. Everybody has his own individual problems. Don't try to pass them on to others. On the contrary, bear the burdens of others. None is your enemy; be ready to bear the burdens of others.○

*Do all the good you can,
in all the ways you can,
in all the places you can,
to all the people you can,
as long as ever you can.*

PARAMAPURUŚA

What is *Puruśa*? He who is lying quiescent is *Puruśa*; He performs no activity. Who is the doer? *Prakrti*, the Operative Principle [creative energy of God]. *Paramapuruśa* is the Cognitive Principle, the witnessing entity. *Puruśa* is acquainted with all that is done by an entity. Whatever the unit mind performs is known to the unit Soul at once; that is, whatever your mind does is known to your *Átma*, your Soul, at once. Whatever action, vice or virtue, is performed by your mind, it creates an impression on the unit Soul, and the impression of the actions on the unit Soul is at once conveyed to the Cosmic Soul.

Whatever action the Cosmic Mind does is not really an action because everything is internal. But whatever the unit mind performs is both internal as well as external. For instance, if a desire for stealing is aroused in your mind, that can be internal when you don't translate it into action. But whatever the Cosmic Mind does is all internal, totally within His mental arena; there is nothing external for Him -- all is within. Whatever He does, He does inside Himself. Without your knowledge He steals away your mind, your Soul. One fine morning you will find that you have lost your mind. Your mind is not existing, as He has stolen it away, and you begin dancing just like a lunatic. How He has managed to steal it away is a mystery to you.

Therefore, He effects everything inside Himself -- everything is within, nothing without. Suppose your boss arrives; you will welcome him and say, "Please come, sit down and have something to eat." You flatter him but inside you speak, "What a trouble has arrived! When will he go?" This is not known to your boss. Thus, two "I"s are within you: one performs action in the external world, and the other is inside. You are well-acquainted with this inner "I", but others do not have the correct information about it. *Sádhana*, therefore, is to unify the two, the internal "I" and the external "I", into one.

Two-ness in one single personality of man is his disease. The greater the gap between these two "I"s, the more you will undergo psychic torment. You must remember that in this second half of the 20th Century there is a great gap between the internal "I" and the external "I". And because of the trouble in adjusting these two "I"s there is an increase in the number of lunatics. This is the greatest disease of the 20th Century.

He is far, far away from him who thinks Him to be remote; and He is nearer than near to him who thinks Him to be close. The man who has eyes to see, who has known Him even a wee bit, knows that He abides in his very sense of existence, in his very heart's desire, as the Supreme Radiance. To seek Him, to attain Him, it is not at all necessary to run from one place to another.

But regarding *Paramapuruśa* there is no double personality. Everything is internal, the entire world is internal for Him. That which is the external world for you is internal for Him. Whatever you think or do in your mind is also internal for Him. He enters your internal world, your mind, and you don't know that He has entered. Entering it, He will steal away your mind and you will not know it.

A man also wants God to steal away his mind. I told you that one of His names is *Makhanchora* ["stealer of butter," one of the names of Lord *Krśńa*]. He will steal away the *Átman* [Soul] of a man and his mind will not know it. As the butter is the essence of the milk, so is the *Átman* the essence of the body. He steals away the *Átman*, so He is *Makhanchora*.

Generally man tells God to come to him, but actually God is already with him. Man is simply unable to see Him. When God appears, the *sádhaka* surrenders himself completely to Him, however, only with his conscious mind. In the most interior corner of his mind he feels that when God appears before him, he will certainly surrender to Him. But along with this he will think that he has been suffering a great deal from asthma, and internally he will seek God's help for its relief. God, Who is in the most interior corner of his mind, knows even this.

This external world, this expressed world which you see, is full of action, full of rhythms. This actional world is both extroversal and introversal for you. There is a world inside your mind -- that is your internal world. And the world which you see without is the extroversal world. Hence this internal world for you is ideational [composed of ideas] and the external world actional. But for *Paramapuruśa* there is nothing like an extroversal world; all is introversal. And hence for Him this world is ideational, His thought projection.

Suppose you have pictured Jodhpur [a town in India] in your mind. This is ideational. But when you look outside, you find that outside it is Jaipur [another town] and not Jodhpur. Then you realize that Jodhpur of your mind is ideational and Jaipur is actual. The same thing occurs in a dream. While you dream you think it to be a fact because the external world does not exist there. For *Paramapuruśa* there is nothing like an extroversal world, and the imaginary internal world which you take to be true in dream is also not here. For Him, the world exists in His ideation. Nothing is extroversal, rather all is introversal. Hence this world is imaginary for Him.

God is a master magician who by His magic spell has created all and has hidden Himself inside His creation. If at all you want to know the creation, the trick of the magician -- this can be done only when you join Him and His party.

This world is ideational for Him, and this ideational cosmos has Him as its center. He is in the center of this all-pervading ideational cosmos. He has to control it. Have you ever seen a fisherman spreading his fishing net in a river? The fisherman spreads the net and he has to manage the net also. Likewise, *Paramapuruśa* has made the ideational world which He only has to manage and control. He controls the ideational world through the energy principles [*guñas*], not directly. For instance, the commander orders the soldiers to catch so-and-so. Then who catches? It is the soldiers, the power of the soldiers. People see that it is the soldier that has caught hold of the man. But the soldier does so only with the direction of his commander. Hence God [*Paramapuruśa*] is just like the commander and *Prakrti* [the Cosmic Energy Principle] is just like the soldier.

The unit mind of man sometimes creates money in the mind, and seeing the mental bank balance, it feels happy. Sometimes man makes himself a Prime Minister and he feels happy -- and sometimes he feels his enemies beaten mentally and he is overjoyed. All this is done only to satisfy his mental hunger, to quench his mental thirst. Ultimately we see that an individual's mental stuff is transformed into worldly objects; it is all directed for personal pleasure, for material pleasure. The flow of the unit mind's mental stuff is called *viśayarasa* [worldly flow] and the flow of the Cosmic Mind is the Supreme Flow. If even once the unit mind happens to come in contact with the Supreme Flow, then material pleasures seem to be dry and insipid, like vegetables without salt. But material objects are needed to maintain one's physical existence. For that, the wise make the worldly flow merge in the Supreme Flow. The wise convert the waves of the worldly flow into the waves of the Supreme Flow. This alone is the way of safety.

Krśńa [the attractor of this ideational world, God] is the nucleus of the Supreme Flow, of the ocean of ideas, and the unit minds are like boats in that great ocean. According to the rise and fall of that Supreme Flow of God the unit minds also rise and fall, as on the waves of the ocean the boat rises and falls. Just so, according to the rise and fall, the unit mind intentionally or unintentionally dances according to the rhythms and waves created by God. This they are bound to do -- there is no help. If someone says that he will not dance because he is ashamed of dancing, it is wrong. Actually he does dance, he simply does not know it. Everybody dances in the ocean of the Supreme Flow; the living beings have to dance. There is no way out. This very dance is the *rasaliilá* of *Krśńa*, the play of the Universal Flow.

Everything in this world of relativity is causal. But for *Paramapuruśa?* He is beyond the scope of relativity. Why is He making the world dance? Why has He made the ocean of Supreme Flow? The answer cannot be found in the world of causality. Why God has done so has no answer because He is beyond the scope of causality. The wise will act to adjust their waves with the waves of His play. They will not try to know why He has done such an action. They will simply try to know Him

Himself. If you have obtained Him, then put the question to Him, "Why have You created this play?"

If you cannot know the cause of a trifling thing like your dancing, how can you know the cause of God's actions? The unit has a very small brain and a very small cranium. It is not possible for him to know God's action. Suppose someone is an M.A. in twenty subjects. If he is asked suddenly to appear in the M.A. examination, he will not pass -- he will have to study again, and then he will be able to appear. This proves that the unit fails to succeed even in its own action. So how can it understand the cause of the play of God? It cannot. The best approach is to love Him, to join His party. If there is true love the Master Magician will certainly make you understand everything, because the more the men of His party know, the more His convenience.

There is a particular rhythm in the Supreme Flow according to the vibration projected in the nucleus of the Supreme Flow. One who becomes acquainted with this does not like the worldly flow any longer, and leaving the worldly flow naturally, he merges into the Supreme Flow. Then the attachment with the rhythms of the worldly flow is lessened and he becomes like a lunatic. People say correctly that *Rádha*, [the great devotee of Lord *Krśńa*], hearing the melodious music of *Krśńa's* flute, started behaving abnormally. This was due to the sudden adjustment of the unit flow with the waves of the Supreme Flow.

A rural boy, when he is brought into the town, watches movies. Then he will no longer like to see rustic plays. He will say, "Those plays are outdated. Cinema is far better." Is it not so? Likewise, when one comes in contact with the waves of The Supreme Flow, the charm of the worldly flow fades away.

Wherever there is vibration, there is sound. The sound of the Supreme Flow is *Krśńa's* flute. The sound of the worldly flow is "Money, more money -- more corn -- more vegetables -- more bank balance." Don't you hear this? The sound of "First Class," the sound of "pension after retirement" are the sounds of the worldly flow. The sound of the "daughter's wedding with no expense" is essentially the sound of the worldly flow. The sound of the Supreme Flow is the flute of *Krśńa*. Hearing this, one no longer appreciates the sound of the worldly flow.

All actions are controlled by the Energy Principle [*Prakrti*] but the Energy Principle is controlled by *Paramapuruśa*, hence *Paramapuruśa* should alone be the be-all and end-all of humans. One must bear it in mind always that the worldly flow of the units is encircled by the Supreme Flow in all the ten directions. You are never away from God, He is with you always, and in no condition are you alone. Since your activity is within the Supreme Flow, whatever you think, whatever you do with your organs, is all made known to God, and since God knows it, it becomes the duty of God as the Witnessing Entity to take you to task. I told you, god is

Whatever you do, God sees everything. For Him no part of your being is closed or shut. He is the innermost part of your being. "Today I am very busy and have to attend a party so I shall do sádhana *for three or four minutes only." He knows that you are placing a party above* sádhana. *He hears both your spoken words as well as the thought words. Actually He hears them first, before they become mental. He is, therefore, in full knowledge of all that goes on within and without and beneath the mind. Don't try to hide anything from Him -- you will not succeed.*

the Creator, the Operator. He has vowed not to punish you, but to correct you. Whatever He thinks proper for you He will do, and it is proper for you too to pray to Him to do this at His will. Whoever has taken His shelter, God will think good of him. He who thinks for his own good by himself will not be helped by God. God will say that he is taking care of himself, so he should continue to do so. But for him who has left himself entirely on God, God has a special responsibility. Therefore it is said that for devotees, God has a special responsibility. It is the duty of God to save the prestige of the devotee, and it is the duty of the devotee to leave everything to Him. Whatever energy is working in the Supreme Flow or in the worldly flow, is under Him. Therefore, when once you have made love with Him, you are not weak, not helpless and not alone. Victory is with you. Remember Him and march ahead -- victory will be yours. You should not be afraid of worldly forces. He who enjoys the highest force of God is sure to succeed. Victory will surely be theirs.

VICTORY TO YOU ALL!

Identify your mind with Him and you will realize that even the minutest objects are you. You are the Pacific Ocean. The universe which is the manifestation of the Cosmic Energy will appear as your own manifestation. The universe which is the play of God also gives Him ecstatic bliss. You meditate on Him and He meditates on you.

OCCULT POWERS OR PARAMAPURUŚA ?

What is the goal of human life? A man should love -- what? *Paramapuruśa*, or occult powers? If one gains occult powers, one may do so many things. In the third stage of *sádhana** a *sádhaka* gets some occult power, and after getting that occult power, suppose he becomes engaged with it, suppose he wants to display it. What will happen? He will fall down. He will be nowhere. He won't remain a *sádhaka*. So in that stage, in the third stage, he will have to be very very cautious. And even with those occult powers he should say, "I want *Paramapuruśa*, not the occult powers." Do you follow?

The mother is cooking and her little baby is there, crying, "Ma, Ma, MA!" What will the mother do at that time? She will give a toy to that little baby and again start her cooking duty. But the baby is quite intelligent and says, "NO! I don't want this toy, I want YOU!" Then

---

**First stage of difficulty; second stage of experience of bliss; third stage of attainment of occult powers; fourth stage of Enlightenment.*

what will the mother do? She will have to do like this [Bábá imitates a mother cuddling a baby in her arms]! It is the mother, and not the toy, that an intelligent baby wants.

Similarly, the occult power is just like a toy. If *Paramapuruśa* gives you a toy, what should you say? Should you say, "Oh, ah, very good, very good!"? No. You should say, "I don't want it, I want YOU." What should you say? "I don't want the toy, I want the MAKER of the toy." So you see the third stage of *sádhana* is a great stage. You'll have to select between occult powers and *Paramapuruśa.*

What will you do in that case [talking to an American disciple], in that third stage of *sádhana*? You will choose occult powers and people will say, "Oh, So-and-so is a supernatural man! So-and-so, you're a great *Yogi*! You have so much power!" Will you do like this? No, no you want *Paramapuruśa*. And you. . .? And you. . .? [asking various disciples] Don't you want occult powers? No, you don't want occult powers. That is right. "I don't want occult powers, I want the Lord of occult powers."

When a *sádhaka* wants occult powers from *Paramapuruśa* he may or may not get occult powers, but it is sure that he will not get *Paramapuruśa* because he did not want *Paramapuruśa*. . .He wanted occult powers so he may or may not get occult powers, but he won't get *Paramapuruśa*. Be very strict in this respect.

[Here Bábá paused for a minute and looked very slowly and intently at everyone in the room. There was absolute silence.]

Do you follow?

Vijay Kumar, stand up. Do you want occult powers? You don't want occult powers? Then you are not an "intelligent" fellow if you don't want occult powers! You don't want to be "intelligent" like that, eh?

Meditate on occult powers and see if you are getting any...what shall I say... *Ánandam* [bliss] or not. Ahhhhh. Now meditate on *Paramapuruśa* -- don't disturb him please... meditate on *Paramapuruśa* [Vijay's head went up]. Certainly you are getting *Ánandam* [bliss].

[Vijay's head went higher, his back arched.] Try to be with *Paramapuruśa*. Go, inner and inner...[Vijay's hands rose up shoulder height, then higher and higher, outstretched and quivering as Bábá talked.]...inner and inner...inner and inner...[Vijay groaned]...inner and inner [Vijay moaning]...inner and inner...[Vijay's moans getting very intense]...BE WITH *PARAMAPURUŚA*.. go inner and inner, inner and inner [Vijay gasped and fell backwards in *samádhi* [estatic trance], into another disciple's lap].

Don't disturb him. He wanted *Paramapuruśa*. So. . .if you want to get occult powers, go outer and outer; if you want *Paramapuruśa*, go inner and inner and inner and inner.

You should always remember this. Don't be after occult powers, be after *Paramapuruśa*. Occult powers, like all other powers, are transitory, temporary in nature, not permanent in nature. As soon as you die, the occult power will be taken away from you. But *Paramapuruśa* will remain with you even at that time, for that property is of a permanent nature.

Occult power is also an ordinary power. The general public does not possess that ordinary power, that's why they think it is a supernatural power. Gold is also an ordinary metal, but because it is a bit rare, that's why it is costly; otherwise machines, spades, tractors would have been manufactured with the help of what? Gold, not iron. It is just like that. Occult power is also an ordinary power, but because it is a bit rare, that's why people say it is supernatural. There is nothing supernatural in this world -- everything is natural.

Do you children want occult powers? Or do you want to be a "fool" like that one [pointing to Vijay, still in an ecstatic state on the floor]? ○

THE LORD'S GRACE IS ALL

Man must be ever-grateful to God. It is He who, out of His Grace, has equipped human beings with the requisites for *sádhana*. He constantly showers the rain of His Grace without reservation even on those persons who gradually degrade themselves towards crudeness. Even though you may condemn God and deny His existence, yet He won't be displeased with you. He will not thrust you on the path of destruction. His imposing countenance of forgiveness will remain ever unchanged. He will always go on directing you how to mend yourself. Who else is your genuine friend and compassionate companion but Him?

> You are my mother, You are my father,
> You are my friend, You are my companion,
> You are my knowledge, You are my wealth,
> You are everything, my Lord of Lords.

O man! Do not disregard this life-giving love of your Supreme Friend. Do not allow any of His gifts to go unused. Pay heed to His words with a steady mind. O man! Do not forget how much He has done for you, how much He is doing, and how ready He is to do anything for you.

When the aspirant advances a little on the path of *sádhana* then the Lord's Grace becomes more and more refulgent in his mind. His mind gets suffused with this feeling of love. The waves of bliss start stirring up his mind. His voice becomes choked with emotions and through his lips, fervent with sentiment, with swaying body and tearful eyes, the devotee's soundless voice recites a feeling of solitary self-surrender to Him, complete dependence on Him --

BRAHMA KRPÁHI KEVALAM

The Lord's Grace is all.

GOD IS WITH YOU

You all know that the *Paramapuruśa* is closest to you. He is so near that nothing can be nearer. As *Paramapuruśa* is everywhere, so He is also at the farthest point from you. If you feel that He is far from you, He becomes so distant that you cannot measure the distance.

If you know that *Paramapuruśa* is great and vast, He appears so huge and enormous that you will be bewildered. He will appear so resplendent that your eyes will close at His sight. He is the Creator of this expressed universe. But He is also in the smallest atom of this universe. If He were not that small, that subtle, how would He enter such a small thing as an atom?

He appears to you according to your feelings towards Him. If you are subtle, He is nearest to you; if you are crude, He is farthest from you. Do you feel whether *Paramapuruśa* is in India or in America? He is so near as to be in your feelings, and so far as to be in a distant country. When you think He is here, He is nearer than here. He is so near that it is difficult to measure the distance. You go searching for Him in the caves of the Himalayas and wander here and there, and He is nowhere. But when you attain awareness of Him, you find that He was along with you in your search. He was seated in your heart.

He shares your joys and pains; He is with you through thick and thin. He never leaves you even when all others have abandoned you.

Every living being is immortal. You have been born in eternity and you are moving towards immortality. Therefore, there is no need to be afraid, despondent, or sorry in any condition.

Never think that your life has become useless. It is in your hands to make your life useful or to waste it. If you are aware that *Paramapuruśa* is always with you, that He is the greatest of entities and there is no other entity which loves you so dearly, you will have no cause to feel that your life has become useless.

It is the utilization of energy which matters and not the possession of an unutilized capacity. Many people have inferiority complexes of different kinds; they think they are not learnéd. How will they achieve their goal of life?

It is wrong to presume that by reading voluminous books or by delivering beautiful lectures, one can attain *Paramapuruśa*. No scholarship, not even literacy is required to meet God. The future of those who are uneducated is also bright.

God's relation with men is a family relation. When parents feed the children, they do not give four pieces of bread to the son who is a Master of Arts and only one to the next son who is only a Matriculate. For parents all their children are equal. Similarly, for God all persons are equal for giving spiritual food. Really, the love of parents is dependent not upon the education of the children but upon the children's attachment for the parents.

The scholars or intellectuals have one drawback. They read different theories and philosophies and these things create a clash in their minds. They are unable to decide whether this or that philosophy is correct. The uneducated, on the other hand, are better; they walk on the spiritual path with steadiness, undisturbed by warring ideas. The intellect is incapable of comprehending *Paramapuruśa*. After all, the intellect is only a creation of the process of *prati-saiṋcara* [evolution] in which consciousness reconverts itself into mind, etc., from the five fundamental factors into which it converted itself earlier. This created thing -- intellect -- therefore cannot comprehend its Creator, the Supreme Being. The puppets can perform any play the master wants them to perform, but they cannot control the man who plays them.

God is also not achieved by a lot of hearing. Some persons are fond of attending many spiritual congregations, but what they hear goes out through the other ear and it does not lead to salvation. With regard to *kiirtan* and the remembering of God, however, it is otherwise. In this field, whether you do it with faith and devotion, or with enmity, either way the results are encouraging. Even when you think of God as an enemy, you are involved in Him. Really, our mind is more activated by anger and hatred. When we have a quarrel with somebody we go on thinking in our mind that the next time we meet him we will say this or that, etc. Therefore, God will be achieved whether you love Him or hate Him. *Rávana* [the enemy of the mythological God-king *Ráma*] was constantly thinking of *Ráma* as his enemy and therefore he also achieved salvation through His hands. But the mere hearing of scriptures or talks is not going to bring about the desired result.

Another point to remember is that God is realized only by those whom He graces with compassion. You should not feel that you have done so much and that God must shower His Grace on you. Rather you should feel that it is up to the Lord to grace you or not. "This body of mine will work like a machine until You grace me with love"; this should be your feeling. If you are proud of

> *One who begs this or that from God is not a devotee, because he wants service from Him. A devotee is one who asks God to utilize his services at His feet. Devotion is service to God.*

your actions, this pride will remain in the end and the Grace of God will not come. For Him all are equal. The virtuous, the thief, the strong, the weak -- all are indistinguishable. For society, the differences matter, but not for God. His Grace is raining on all, but if you are carrying an umbrella of ego on your head, how will you get drenched by His Grace? Everyone has a right to enter the realm of Pure Consciousness [*Brahma loka*]; this is the birthright of all men. He is kind to all every moment of one's life. One has only to receive this kindness by removing the ego.

However great a sinner may be, the moment he surrenders to the Lord, he becomes a devotee -- his salvation is guaranteed. The Person whom you are trying to achieve -- the *Paramapuruśa* -- is your own innermost Self. Your relation with Him is not external, to be defined by courts, laws or society. It is a family relationship. The desire to meet God is not a unilateral affair. It is a mutual thing. You walk one step towards Him and He will come twenty towards you.

When an infant starts walking, the parent first asks him and goads him to walk a little. He tries to walk, but falls. Then the parent advances and lifts him up in his lap. So also, God. Make the slightest efforts and He will pick you up and place you in His lap. Your relation with God is personal. No one can sever this relationship. It is part of your being, your birthright.

There is a famous verse from the *Upaniśads* [spiritual scriptures] which says that you cannot reach *Paramapuruśa* unless you are strong and full of energy. The word *bala* means that spiritual force which functions at the base of a living being. In ordinary parlance, however, *bala* means "capacity." It depends upon the extent to which one makes use of one's spiritual, psychic, and physical energy. A person may have immense capacity, but to the extent that he does not utilize it, it does not become helpful in God-realization. *Bala*, therefore, depends on the extent of the use of one's capacity.

When the divine bridge was constructed by *Ráma* to cross the ocean, *Hanumán*, the giant monkey, brought mountains, but the squirrel brought only small pebbles. Both were equally strong and full of energy, as each was working to its full capacity. Thus, even a comparatively weaker man can become *balván* [strong] by utilizing the small energy he has. Whatever power, energy, you have, utilize it for *sádhana* and service, and you are *balván*, fit to reach *Paramapuruśa*. None of you need, therefore, despair. Everyone has the requisite wherewithal to reach the Almighty.

The utilization of energy should be in the proper direction. If you have to move to the East and you start moving towards the West, that action will be considered full of madness. *Ánanda Márga* has the correct way through subjective approach and objective adjustment. While the followers of *Ánanda Márga* keep their eyes steadily on the Absolute, they do not ignore this relative world either. They work for self-realization and social upliftment, and hence the utilization of their energy is never in vain. When the effort is correct and the utilization proper, you will certainly reach the goal. I do not want you to wait life after life to reach your goal. You should realize the goal in this very life. Why will you waste even one precious moment of this life? Therefore, fear not! Success is yours for the asking! Go on making the correct effort!

The primary aim of every spiritual aspirant is not to enjoy the nectar of devotion by himself but to distribute it all around. He is eager to share with others the bliss which he enjoys.

In ancient times there was one such devotee who used to go from place to place distributing the bliss of devotion. His name was *Nárada*. Once he asked *Paramapuruśa*, "O Lord, all scholars and philosophers say that You are omniscient, but people do not feel your presence everywhere. Which, therefore, is the place where Your presence can most be felt? Which place do you consider as dearest to You?"

The Lord replied, "It is true that I am everywhere; there is no action, no thought, no feeling in which I am not present. All actions take place before My eyes, within My mind. Nothing can be done or thought which is meant to be hidden from Me. Still, I do not live in the seventh heaven as people think. The minds which are free from narrowness and limitations are the places dearest to me. The true meaning of the word *Yoga* is to unify. But those who do *ásana*, *práńáyáma*, etc. without devotion are cultivating the desert. Without the water of devotion, their efforts will not succeed. I am not in the heart of such dry *Yogis*."

The meaning of the word *bhakti* is attraction for the Supreme. When the attraction is for something limited, it is called *asakthi*; when the attraction is for the Supreme, it is devotion, *bhakti*. There is no compromise, no meeting point between *asakthi* and *bhakti*, between the attraction for the Supreme and for the objects of the world. In *asakthi* the feeling is that I get that object. In *bhakti* the feeling is that I merge myself in Him. Where there is no desire, there the Lord lives. The Lord and desire for the world cannot coexist, like the sun and the night.

For devotees all other enjoyments are insipid. They are like saltless food. Hence, the Lord says, "Where my devotees sing My praises and do *kiirtan*, there I go -- I cannot help going there."

Someone is scholarly; another is rich. They may be devotees or they may not be. The only thing the devotee needs is love of the Lord. When all feelings, all attachments are directed towards Him, it is devotion. The only qualification is a sincere heart. If your heart is pure, you need nothing else.

Nothing is gained by becoming a man of knowledge [*jiṇáni*]; this has use only so far as devotion is not born. When you eat tasty food, the paper on which you place this food is knowledge [*jiṇána*]. The food itself is action [*karma*], and the taste of the food is devotion [*bhakti*]. If you have absorbed the food and tasted it, the dirty paper of *jiṇána*, knowledge, has to be thrown into the dust bin. This alone is wisdom. Be wise! ○

> *The life center or nucleus of all emotions and ideas is He -- that Supreme Soul, that Soul of souls. Concentrate on that characteristic self. You have come into the field of* sádhana *in order to enter the kingdom of light beyond the shores of darkness. May your journey to the Empyreal region be glorious and triumphant. Bon voyage to you!*

God is the controller of that vital force which keeps the organisms alive. He is our friend who saves us from the jaws of calamities by His affectionate and tender touch. He exists everywhere. He is present about us sometimes as sound expression, sometimes as thought or emotion, and then again sometimes as individual entities. There is not a place in the universe where His Entity is not manifest. What we apparently take to be a void is also full of His Entity. He is even where the human intellect cannot reach, and where the imagination bounds back, thwarted and baffled. In the planetary world it is His glory that shines as the sun. The backbone of the nervous system, the praising of the dead ancestors, the truth of the sages, the controller, the friend, the sun -- are all these separate entities? No, all is He, all is He, all is He.

KNOWLEDGE

The greatest knowledge a man can acquire in the realm of physicality and mentality is that all the knowledge acquired by him so far is false.

Physical knowledge is like that leaf of the shala tree on which people take meals. As long as you have not eaten, the leaf has value, but the moment you have finished your meal, the leaf goes into the dust bin to be licked by the street dogs. When you come to realize that this physical knowledge of yours is worth licking by a dog, then devotion will arise in you, then you will acquire true knowledge. For acquiring real knowledge, spiritual knowledge, *Paramapuruśa* should be made the goal of your life.

How is it possible to make *Paramapuruśa* the goal of your life? *Paramapuruśa* is the subject for the whole cosmos, and the cosmos is His object. He is the Supreme Subjectivity; you are His object. It is not possible to make Him your object as you are His object. Then what are you to do? You have to take the ideation that He is always witnessing you. The wise do not take *Paramapuruśa* as their object; they think that they are being witnessed by Him. *Paramapuruśa* is not my object, but I am the object of *Paramapuruśa*. When this feeling is felt constantly by a man, all the time, this stage is called *Dhruvasmrti* [constant remembrance]. You know that you are the object of *Paramapuruśa*, but you do not remember it all the time. When through *sádhana* a man never forgets that *Paramapuruśa* is always witnessing him -- this is called *Dhruvasmrti*. In this stage alone a man attains true knowledge. This spiritual knowledge can be translated into the mental sphere as well as into the physical sphere. If a man is willing to do so, he should, for he will do a great deal of good for the world. This alone is the real knowledge. With this alone, progress is possible. The greatest learned man is he who understands that he is not at all learned.

This very spiritual knowledge alone is devotion. Knowledge finally transforms itself into devotion after constant effort. That is, when knowledge realizes that nothing is to be effected by it, then alone it surrenders to devotion. When knowledge surrenders to devotion, that is spiritual knowledge. Remember that once you have devotion, you have everything. If *Paramapuruśa* asks you for your request, you should request nothing at all --and if at all God is pleased to give you something, you should ask for absolute devotion.○

PRIDE AND ITS CURE

Jñāna, karma and bhakti [knowledge, action, and devotion] are essential for the attainment of God, the cherished goal of life. It is through knowledge and action that devotion is aroused, which leads man to that Supreme Bliss. While devotion is free from any defect, knowledge and action may create some shortcomings. Acquisition of knowledge often makes a man lazy and proud, while *karma* may make a man proud. Unless a spiritual aspirant is able to get rid of these defects, he cannot be established in *kevala bhakti* [complete devotion] which is absolutely essential for the attainment of God. Wise men will, therefore, adopt a conduct to save themselves from the evil effects of knowledge and action.

It has been observed that those engaged in the acquisition of knowledge lose touch with practicality. Their constant preoccupation with books makes them lazy and lethargic and they become shy of work. This eventually leads to their downfall. The golden rule of getting rid of one's defects is that one should create an opposite feeling in the mind and bring it into execution. Therefore, in order to avoid laziness one will have to work hard. Work is the manifestation of the Supreme Entity and so everyone will have to work and work in ever larger and larger measure. Work here does not mean any engagement which yields no result. Work is work only when it is directed towards the collective welfare. This alone will save one from the evils of laziness and lethargy. The pride which creeps in due to acquisition of knowledge also has very serious repercussions in human life. It can lead to the complete downfall of the individual. Pride is mainly of three types, and each of these has disastrous results.

The first type of pride is conceit, which arises when a person thinks that he deserves more than what he is getting, which causes him to develop an overbearing attitude towards everyone. Anyone who indulges in this loses his discriminating judgment just as a drunkard does. A man is different from an animal only because he possesses discrimination and intellect. Just as a drunkard gradually loses this priceless quality, a prideful man also becomes bereft of this faculty. Since the loss of the rational faculty is against cardinal human virtues, drinking is a sin. Similarly pride is also a sin and leads to the downfall of the individual.

Self-aggrandizement is the second type of pride. Being puffed up with vanity, the person wants to project his image in an exaggerated manner. Often we hear a person saying that he has a rose the size of a balloon in his garden when the actual rose may be the size of a pingpong ball. Constant indulgence in this type of activity converts the mind into crudity.

The third type of pride is prestige, which is the desire to make oneself known. Such a man expects attention from everyone and hankers after name and fame. This mental state can be easily compared with the mental condition of the beggar. The beggar asks for money from others, but a person craving for prestige begs others to give him respect. Such a desire is really meaningless and possesses no value.

Having analyzed the various types of pride and their evil effects, it is necessary to examine the ways and means of getting rid of these defects. *Caetanya Mahāprabhu* [a great saint of India] has given a psychological method for saving oneself from the malady of pride. Pride is really a mental ailment, and persons suffering from this disease require a regular psychological treatment. In order to get rid of pride one will have to inculcate the habit of being polite and humble. Just as a straw remains lying on the ground but by remaining humble does not lose its importance, similarly a man will never become insignificant by being humble. Only humility like that of the straw will save a person from pride.

To avoid pride it is also necessary to have forbearance and tolerance like that of a tree which, though being cut, continues to give its cool shade. A person who is always engaged in the thought of his own prestige must learn how to think of others' prestige. He must never forget that respect begets respect and that he should always honor those who are not being honored by anyone. This constant practice will remove the evil effects of the desire for prestige. The easiest method of doing this is to do *namaskár* [greeting] first and not create a situation in which you do the responding greeting.

A man moving about puffed up with vanity and arrogance and always engaging in self-aggrandizement can improve only by utilizing his time in *kúrtan*. If he keeps himself engaged in *kúrtan* he will not get time to criticize and scandalize anyone in order to elevate himself by comparison. So it is a must for such a person to do *kúrtan* to the maximum so that he does not get time to indulge in the nefarious activity of criticism.

Therefore, a spiritual aspirant who has set God as his goal must always strive to get rid of lethargy and pride, and gain the full benefits of knowledge; he must work so as to arouse and enliven devotion, which is the only road to the journey's end. He will have to engage himself in the collective welfare, practice the qualities of humility, forbearance, and tolerance, learn to honor those who are not honored by anyone, and participate in and organize *kúrtan*. ○

> *One will not be able to know anything unless one develops the psychology of "I know not." It is the fundamental spirit of a true aspirant.*

LONGING FOR THE GREAT

Each and every living being has longing for the Great. Each and every man wants to do something noble, something lasting. But the life of each and every man is not crowned with success, because the thing that a man requires most is proper guidance.

There was a *Yogi* king in ancient India about 3500 years ago and his guide was Lord *Kṛṣṇa*. *Kṛṣṇa* was a great *Yogi*. The name of that *Yogi* king was *Yudhisthira*. *Yudhi* means "in war, in battle," and *sthira* means "unaffected, unassailed, balanced." "He who can maintain his mental balance even in wartime" is *Yudhisthira*. Now, who is a *Yogi*? *Yogi* means a practical man. A *Yogi* has little to do with theory. A *Yogi* is not a theoretician. He is a practical man.

King *Yudhisthira* was asked a question, and that question was, "What is the proper path, the proper way?" His answer was that one is to follow the practical man and not the theoretician. The theory may or may not be a success in the field of application. It may be good in books, it may be good in theory, it may be good in contemplation, but it may or may not be useful in practical life. So a *Yogi*, a spiritual aspirant, is to follow the practical man. This means a *Yogi* is to follow a *Maháyogi*, a great *Yogi*.

Now, there are so many scriptures in the world but these scriptures vary from one another. The supporters of these scriptures, the supporters of each and every scripture say, "Ours is the message of God. It cannot be challenged." By saying this, that it cannot be challenged, they try to block the intellectual progress of the human society. They say that a man should not think beyond this. They are enemies of human progress, they are enemies of human civilization. Had there been no intellectual progress, then even in this second half of the twentieth century, we would have been in the stone age. So there must be intellectual progress, and no power, no theory should try to block this progress. But scriptures vary from one another, and the supporters of each and every scripture say, "Ours is the message of God; it is the Supreme Word." Then, if all the scriptures are messages of that same Supreme Being, why do they vary from one another? The Supreme Being is one, and if those scriptures are messages of that single Supreme Being, then there should not be any variation amongst themselves. This proves that these scriptures are not the messages of the Supreme Being.

What should a common man do? Whom to follow? In a particular scripture it says that during meditation, a *sádhaka* should be facing East. Another scripture will say no, a *sádhaka* should be facing West. Now, how to adjust? Well, if a *sádhaka* wants to make an adjustment, he has to face North or South!

A very difficult job and a knotty problem. A very knotty problem! Now, the spiritual scriptures vary from one another. A common man. . .what is a common man to do? Scriptures vary, social codes also vary. In ancient times, there were so many social systems, and now there are so many social systems in different portions of the world and amongst different races of the world and amongst different races of a particular country. In the same country, there are so many social codes and social usages. Whom to follow? Which one is the absolute? Which one is perfect? What is a common man to do? A very knotty problem. What to do and what not to do? We see that the intellectuals always quarrel amongst themselves. Non-intellectual people may have love and affection amongst themselves, but intellectuals, you know, learned people, always quarrel amongst themselves. They think that if a particualr intellectual supports the views of another intellectual it is an insult to his prestige! The intellectual thinks he should create a particular school of thought of his own -- he should not support others. So intellectuals always quarrel amongst themselves.

Whom is the common man to follow? Mr. A intellectual says that Mr. B intellectual knows nothing, and the latter says that another intellectual, Mr. C, knows nothing. What should the common man do and whom to follow? Mr. A, Mr. B, or Mr. C? A knotty problem. We see that the intellectuals always vary. Now what is a man to do? What is a common man, a practical man, a *Yogi,* to do?

Yudhisthira was a *Yogi* king. He says, "Now what is the supreme goal of life? The supreme physical, intellectual, mental and spiritual goal of the entire cosmological order is the same, the same desideratum for all. Where lies that desideratum? Who is that Supreme Point? What is that Supreme Terminus? What is that Supreme Culminating Point and where lies that Supreme Point?"

He says the essence of spirituality lies hidden in the "I-feeling" of each and every individual. When "I" is connected with some other physical object, when "I" is related to some other physical being, then that physical being is the object, "I" is the subject, and that connecting link is the verbal expression. "I". . ."water". . ."drinking." "I am drinking water." The "am drinking" is the connecting link: subject, object and connecting link.

Now there is an "I" in each and every living being. There is an "I" in you. "I am going." "I am seeing

Bábá" -- Each and every individual has an "I". That "I" is connected with external physicalities, with external objects. Now when "I" is connected with external objects, that "I" is the subtlest portion of mind. "I exist." While saying "exist," indirectly we say, "I exist in this world," exist in such-and-such place." The object is mute here; the object is not expressed but the object is understood. This "I" of "I exist" is the subtlest portion of mind.

Now you know that in the mind of each and every living being is this feeling of "I exist." "I am, I exist." This "I" is the subtlest mind. But don't you know that there is the feeling of "I exist" in you? You know it. You know this fact, that there is the feeling of "I exist" in you. Don't you know it? Then "I know the fact that I exist.I know the fact that there is a feeling of "I exist" in me." Now here, the "I" of "I exist", the subject of the sentence "I exist", is the subtlest mind. And the "I" of "I know", the subject of the sentence "I know that I exist", is the *Átman*, is the Spirit, is the SOUL. It is not the mind. There is the feeling of "I exist" in me. "I exist" -- that is the subtlest mind. And the feeling that "I exist" is in me, is known to me. That knowing "I" [I know that I exist], the "I" of "I know", is the *Átman*, the Spirit, the Soul.

Now this "I exist" is the subtlest mind and it is called *guhá* in Sanskrit. And what is the essence of spirituality? The "I" of "I know." "I know that I exist." That "I" of "I know" is the essence of spirituality.

You know so many things, but you have to know your Self. When you know your Self, that stage, that stance, is the Supreme Stance; your *sádhana*, your spiritual practice is for that realization, to know your own "I". You try to know so many people but you do not know your Self. It is just like the citizen of Manila who wants to see Hongkong, wants to see Tokyo or Rangoon, but he does not know Manila. First, know Manila, first know your own Self. First know your inner "I".

You know, a man can easily become omniscient. How can a living creature, a living being be omniscient? The secret is, if you want to know all, know one, and that one is your own "I". And if you want to know everything, if you try to know everything, you won't be able to know anything. If you want to know all, know one and that one is your own "I". The spirit of *dharma*, the spirit of spirituality, the spirit of *Yoga*, is hidden in what? In your own "I" feeling, in your own "I exist." It lies in your own "I" feeling because the "I" of "I know" lies hidden in the "I" of "I exist."

Who is your nearest person? You try to know so many things, but you should know first of all your nearest object. What is your nearest object? Hands? Fingers? No, no, no...Arms? No, no, no...Chest? No, no, no...What is the nearest point? Your "I" is your nearest entity. And the distance cannot be measured. Can you measure it? It cannot be measured. So it is the nearest entity. First of all you should know, you should come in close contact with all the characteristics of your own "I". In your books, in your laboratories, you try to learn the characteristics of oxygen, nitrogen, hydrogen monoxide, hydrogen peroxide, and so many elements and compounds, but you don't know the characteristics of your nearest object. Try to know all the characteristics of your nearest object in your mental laboratory.

So how to do it? In the laboratory, a theroetician won't be of any help, won't be able to help you in your research. You require a practical demonstrator there in the laboratory. So, King Yudhisthira says, in the realm of spirituality, in the realm of *Yoga*, whom to follow? Not those scriptures. You may or may not follow the scriptures, you may or may not follow those social codes and you may or may not follow those intellectuals. What you are to do is to follow those practical demonstrators; that means you are to follow the *Yogis*. And certainly according to His direction, you will attain that Supreme Stance, and you will enjoy that Supreme Beatitude. ○

THE HIGHEST DEVOTEE

Different kinds of *sádhakas* inhabit this world. Some ardently desire liberation [*mukti*] while others do not. The latter type base their choice on the reasoning that by becoming one with God, the *sádhaka* loses the pleasure of being next to Him and harbouring Him as his sole ideation in work, service and sacrifice. Little do they know that this very ideation of the Cosmic will lead them to liberation, for their minds have Him for their object.

The best and highest *sádhaka* and devotee, however, surrenders the decision of this question to God. The ideation that he embraces is: "I am at Your disposal. It is up to You to plan what You like for me." His is the wisdom to foresee that complete surrender alone, which is the essence of the highest devotion, will enable him to sail the sea of existence -- unto His Feet! ○

ONE AND ZERO

Your every action should be with *Paramapuruṣa*. Without Him, all your actions are as nothing, no matter how great they may seem. Yet if you do even a little with Him, you will have done a lot. He is like the number one, and your actions are like zeroes. If you take the One (1) first, and to that One perform your actions, it is like adding zeroes to the One, it is like multiplying by ten with each action. But if that One is not there, your zeroes are added to each other and the net result is only zero.

So go on multiplying; do not let all be zero. You have taken a human form to realize Him, let not your life be wasted.

So, I say, get the intuitional knowledge from a proper preceptor. You can learn this through empirical knowledge. Intuitional knowledge cannot be gained from books. For this, one has to go to a preceptor with devotion and reverence. Try to awaken devotional bent and bias. It will come to you, if you so wish. Once devotion is awakened, you shall get God's mercy without any doubt.

BHAKTI: DEVOTION

The word *bhakti* [devotion] means worshipping. For worshipping both the person who worships and He who is worshipped must be present. For this reason, as long as there is difference between the devotee and God, there is the opportunity and necessity of *bhakti sádhana*.

Bhakti means longing for the Supreme. Now the question arises if *bhakti* is natural or unnatural for living beings. All the conscious or crude things we see in the manifested universe bear attraction for one another. This attraction alone is the *dharma* [nature] of the created universe, and as a consequence, the continuity of the thought-projections of the Cosmic Mind is maintained. Therefore I say that attraction is natural for everything. It is on account of the mutual attraction of myriads of heavenly bodies oscillating in the infinite space that balance is maintained in the firmament. There is effort for self-preservation. The bee flies around and around flowers in quest of honey, just for the sake of preserving its existence. It can be seen that every entity runs toward that abode which is more lasting and secure and which can provide it greater and longer safety. People run after money for the only reason that they believe that they can maintain their lives under the shelter of money; that is to say, money alone can save them. But they do not know that money can provide them neither permanent stability nor a securely-founded shelter. Even during the span of their lives, money will come and go several times. At times its glamor will dazzle their eyes, and sometimes it will make them cry, hunger-stricken.

Not to speak of money alone, all finite objects have this characteristic. What is not infinite cannot permanently remain the object of your enjoyment. It cannot be your permanent resort, since the existence of all these finite objects is dependent on others, bounded by the limits of time, place and person.

If the terrific speed with which the extroverted man runs after finite objects is introverted toward the Supreme Being of his life, he can attain *Brahma*, he can achieve the Supreme State. The devotee recites: "O Almighty, may the attraction which the ignorant man bears towards the objects of his mind become an eternal love for Thee, through Thy remembrance."

You understand for certain that pure *bhakti* cannot be based on finite objects, since these cause extroverted feelings. But I observe painfully that many men confine their love and devotion to finite objects.

What is the result? They do not attain the pervasiveness which love confers. They do not realize that every minutest atom of this vast universe is a creative manifestation of that very Cosmic Consciousness, His grand expression. They spend millions on the installation of idols but ignore the afflictions of the suffering humanity.

The world is a changing phenomenon. Therefore, it is unwise to be attached to any object in this ever-changing world. The very name and form will undergo changes with the change in time and place. The child changes into youth, the youth into the old, and the old into the corpse. But if wise men take every object of the world as the expression of the one and single Cosmic Consciousness, then on seeing the changes in the name and form of any particular object, they will not be affected by pain or pleasure. Cosmic Consciousness to them would remain Cosmic Consciousness; they would lose nothing.

The methods and kinds of *bhakti Yoga* are manifold. Man adopts the process of *bhakti sádhana* according to his own nature.

CRUDE DEVOTION [*támasika bhakti*]: The persons craving finite pleasures instead of Supreme Bliss and who are under the influence of violence, arrogance or jealousy, are crude *sádhakas*.

MUTATIVE DEVOTION [*rajasika bhakti*]: Those carrying on spiritual practices with the goal of attaining a particular finite object are called mutative *sádhakas*. Mutative *sádhakas* are engrossed in realizing their selfish ends, while not causing harm to others. They are worshipping the Lord in a crude way with flowers and leaves for the sake of worldly objects, fame or wealth; they in fact long for those objects and not for the Lord.

SENTIENT DEVOTION [*sattvik bhakti*]:Those who pursue their practice with the prayer, "O Lord, may my *karma* be annihilated. Emancipate me from the cycle of birth and death"; those who pursue their practice as their duty; and also those who pursue it for the fear that people may decry them, are classed as sentient *sádhakas*. Inasmuch as they do not seek attainment of the Supreme, even this *sattvika sádhana* cannot be termed as a superior *sádhana*, or as the Supreme *sádhana*, because none of these motives control the energies of the aspirants and direct them towards the adored, the Supreme *Brahma*. The aim of the aspirant is channeled in a different direction; he carries on with an inferior goal. All these three, crude, mutative and sentient types of devotion are inferior devotion.

UNQUALIFIED DEVOTION [*nirguña bhakti*]: Here the aspirant has no other object; he betakes himself toward the Supreme *Brahma* only by the urge of his own spirit. If questioned why he loves Him and devotes himself towards Him, then he says in reply, "Oh, why do I love? I do not know. I love Him just because I like to love Him. Should I not love? He is the Life of my life, the Soul of my soul."

COMPLETE DEVOTION [*kevala bhakti*]: If the aspirant from the very outset realizes the permanence of unqualified devotion, the questions like "What have I attained?" "What do I wish to attain?" etc., do not arise in his mind. This is the culmination of *bhakti*. If there is undivided knowledge with the object, then there exists one and only one entity, and that is why such devotion is called *kevala bhakti*. *Kevala bhakti* is not attained by baths, exercises or efforts. Those who have not been blessed with Divine Grace even in the least cannot have any realization about it.

In the discussion of *bhakti*, the use of the word "*bháva*" [spiritual ideation] is indispensable. What does *bháva* signify?

Bháva is that whereby the mindstuff [*citta*] becomes purged and dominated by the sentient principle, brilliant with the rays of the sun of love. As a result of the *bháva*, man directs his natural attractive forces towards the adored. But here the adored is not outside him; the adored is the life of his life, the mind of his mind and the life-master of his entire existence. When this feeling of devotion for the adored awakens the introversion of his tendencies, then he becomes absorbed with this *bháva*. He attains the state of self-realization.

When there is fear, or any crude propensities in the mind, there cannot be pure *bhakti*. The devotion generated through fear is no *bhakti* at all, it is but a lamentable state of mental crudeness.

Some for fear of hell, and some for fear of torture and retribution in the next life pray to the Lord, and in particular, hunger for salvation. This betrays lack of knowledge of the truth. You should not give encouragement to this inferiority complex. Those who accept or know the Lord as their own Self have no reason to entertain any fear of Him. This very fearless movement toward the Lord is termed love.

When the mind attains Supreme serenity, and when a feeling of affection is developed for all beings, the sages call it love. Love cannot be developed for anything mean or finite. Love and passion are mutually antagonistic tendencies. The attachment for a finite thing is an expression of extroverted energy, whereas the attraction for the Infinite is an expression of introverted energy. That is why these two can never coexist. The aspirant will, therefore, have to skillfully transform passion into love. Do you love your son?? No, no, you do not love your son. You love *Brahma* in the form of your son. By loving your son as a son, you cannot love the Lord. Where there is the feeling of son, there is no Lord; and where there is the Lord, there is no son. Where you exist, He does not, and where He exists, you are no more.

Now this sádhana *which is* sádhana *for complete merger, for unification, starts with fearful love. Love must be there. Unless and until there is love there cannot be unification. So love must be there but it starts with fearful love and ends in fearless love; and the space between fearful love and fearless love is the space of* sádhana. *What is* sádhana? Sádhana *is the transformation of fearful love into fearless love.*

There are three grades of devotees: inferior, intermediate and superior devotees. Those bearing neither knowledge nor earnestness are inferior devotees. Those who have reverence but have no knowledge of the *shástras* [scriptures, philosophy], are the intermediate type of devotees. Those versed in the *shástras*, competent in *sádhana* practices, and of firm mind are the devotees of the highest degree. *Kevala bhakti* is attainable only by the highest grade of devotees. They alone attain the infinite evolution of their soul.

Therefore, O devotees! Remember the Lord's name, else all your efforts shall be reduced to zero. Under all circumstances and amid all activities, firmly cling to His name. The *dharma* of your childhood is to study and to practice *Brahma sádhana*; and the *dharma* of youth is to earn money and to practice *Brahma sádhana*, and the *dharma* of your old age when you become incapacitated for all crude physical activities, is the practice of *Brahma sádhana* alone.

The true devotees love the world, society and everything around because they perceive each and every manifestation of the artful *Prakrti* [creative energy] with a feeling full of the single Universal Spirit. They love the finite too as a portion of the Universal. They love worldly pleasures as divine bliss, varied by time, place and person. They keep their minds absorbed in the eternal currents of the divine flow. Such devoted aspirants alone are the true enjoyers, and their object of enjoyment is the

Supreme *Brahma*.

The aspirants of *bhakti* surrender their all to their Adored. Everything objective is inside the mind; hence if the mind itself is surrendered to *Brahma*, everything automatically becomes surrendered.

"The universe is Thy abode, the supreme *Prakrti* [creative energy] herself is Thy consort. O Lord, thou needest nothing. Then, O Lord, what can I offer Thee? O yes, yes! I remember one thing. Thy true devotees have snatched away Thy mind. Thou needest one thing -- Thy mind is lost. O Lord, I offer my mind to Thee. Grace me by Thy acceptance." O

When the devotional depth comes, love, too will be brimming with high sentiments, full and over-flowing. In that stage alone will come your final realization of the Supreme Consciousness. Where "I" is, "He" is not...where "He" is, "I" is not. Remember, devotion is the prerequisite of sádhana. *Maturity of devotion is love, and maturity of love is HE.*

THE MISSION OF BECOMING PERFECT

In this world nothing is non-causal. Everything has a cause. The fact that you have been born as a human being also has a cause and a purpose. You may not know it, but the Supreme Being knows it.

Life is movement from imperfection to perfection. When inanimate objects become animate there is progress. There is further progress when animate beings become multicellular metazoic organisms, more and more complicated structures. Man is the highest being, the being most perfect in structure. Man is thus a perfected animal. But this is the beginning of progress for man. He still has to achieve further physical, intellectual and spiritual perfection.

Movement towards perfection -- God -- is *dharma*. Movement towards imperfection is *adharma*. The former is life, the latter is death. Man's movement towards animality is therefore not life, it is death.

No movement is free from friction or obstacles.

Even when you walk, the force of gravity obstructs you. Movement towards perfection is obstructed by all the forces of imperfection, of evil. The sinful, the crude, the narrow obstruct all movement for the expansion of man's mind. But perfection being a God-ward movement, do not be afraid -- move on. Obstacles will go down the drain, where they belong. You will progress.

The mission of man's life is to move towards perfection, towards God. This is his *dharma*, his duty. In this struggle the forces of evil are bound to be defeated. This has been the case all along, and history will repeat itself.

You have no right to rest until you have fulfilled your mission of being perfect, of being divine, of establishing yourself in perfection. Rest is sin as it puts a stop to this movement. Do not rest until you have reached the goal.

TAKING REFUGE AT HIS FEET

Nothing is outside Him. He who seeks Him is really wise, for attaining Him means attaining all.

There is a beautiful story in the *Rámáyana* [an Indian epic]. Once *Ráma* and *Lakśamana* [the god-king and his brother] were sailing in a boat across the Ganges. As the story goes, the boat turned into gold at the touch of *Ráma's* feet. When the boat reached the other bank, the wife of the boatman came to know about this miracle. She brought all the timbers from her house and started turning them into gold by touching them to *Ráma's* feet. Seeing the foolishness of his wife, the boatman told her, "Look here, how long are you going to toil like this? Act wisely. Take refuge under those feet that have such miraculous power. If you do so, you will be able to turn any worldly object into gold at will."

Taking His refuge means merging one's egoistic vanity in Him. The attainment of God is difficult for those who want to work out the profit and loss of "What shall I get out of this attainment?" If a man, while surrendering himself to Him, is conscious of his petty ego's profit and loss, then how can he dedicate his petty ego to Him? His worm-eaten mental flower shall not be worthy of His worship. Entertaining no desire for sensuous happiness, a man has to surrender himself to the waves of the flow of that inscrutable Supreme Fountainhead -- God.

He makes you do sádhana, *furnishes you with intellect and strength -- surrender yourself to His will. Off with your load of self-conceit. Lighten the burden of your life and let yourself drift on the course of His will. It is He who is teaching you* sádhana *in the guise of a* Guru. *You are plundering His mercy through everything day and night. Go on working selflessly like a machine, leaving the doer-ship to Him. How little can your small intellect comprehend His inscrutable* liilá*! How little can it be analyzed! So, instead of analyzing His* liilá, *only keep the bearing of that inscrutable juggler ever aglow before your eyes.*

THE LORD'S FEET

Tripurásura, the father of *Gayásura*, was a great devotee of Lord *Viśńu* [a mythological god]. Many devotees of Lord *Shiva* [a great *Yogi* worshipped as the Lord] wanted him to become a devotee of *Shiva* instead. But how could *Tripurasura* go against his *Iishta* [beloved goal of life]? "Though I know that there is no difference between *Viśńu* and *Shiva*, for me everything is Lord *Viśńu*, for He is my *Iishta*."

But the devotees of Lord *Shiva* still put pressure on *Tripurásura*, in order to see him also become a devotee of *Shiva*. His conversion might have been possible if the worshippers of *Shiva* had made a logical appeal to *Tripurásura's* understanding that there is actually no difference between Lord *Shiva* and Lord *Viśńu*, and that both are only the functional counterparts of *Paramapuruśa*. But under the pressure put on him by the devotees of Lord *Shiva*, *Tripurásura* initiated a crusade against all the devotees of Lord *Shiva*, until he finally came upon *Shiva* Himself. But however powerful *Tripurásura* was, how could he fight against Lord *Shiva*?

He was defeated by Lord *Shiva* and met his death.

After the death of *Tripurásura*, his son, *Gayásura*, became the king. He, too, was a devotee of Lord *Viśńu*. He worshipped Him with all his heart and devotion, and finally succeeded in attaining a boon of immortality: not to be killed by man, demon or god, in earth, heaven or hell, by day, night, evening or morning. Endowed with such a great power, *Gayásura* went all over the world conquering people, torturing them and making their lives miserable. None were spared -- not even the devotees of *Viśńu* or *Shiva*.

But as the saying goes, "Power corrupts, and absolute power corrupts absolutely." *Gayásura*, who had received his power from Lord *Viśńu*, thought to defeat the Lord Himself. Is not the tamboura [a musical instrument used by *Shiva*] a fool if it thinks that the persons bowing before the Lord are, in fact, paying respect to it? *Gayásura* started thinking that the great power he possessed was actually his power. He finally challenged Lord *Viśńu*, and since *Viśńu* Himself had granted the boon, how could it fail? *Viśńu* was defeated by *Gayásura*. *Gayásura* bound *Viśńu* to a tree and then went all over the world with a very bloated ego.

When things had become intolerable for the people, they approached Lord *Viśńu*, still tied to the tree, and recounted their miseries, requesting Him to do something. *Viśńu* pleaded helplessness, as He Himself was in a precarious condition! Then the devotees reminded the Lord that He had given the boon of immortality to *Gayāsura* in the physical realm only. The devotees urged Lord *Viṡṅu* to use His psychic and spiritual power to defeat *Gayāsura*, and relieve the people of their miseries. Lord *Viṡṅu* assured them that He would do something in the matter.

When *Gayāsura* returned to Lord *Viṡṅu* to offer his prayers, *Viṡṅu* said, *"Gayāsura!* I once gave you what you asked, and you have defeated me. You should now give me a boon." *Gayāsura* readily agreed to it. *Viṡṅu* then asked that *Gayāsura* be turned into stone. *Gayāsura* had no alternative but to say, "So be it."

Gradually *Gayāsura's* legs started turning to stone. When he was stone up to his waist, he said, "Wait! I have three conditions!" His first condition was that the Lord put His two feet in *Gayāsura's* heart. The Lord agreed to it, but askĕd the reason for such a condition.

Gayāsura said, "So that people should know that the feet of the Lord are always in the heart of a devotee, good or bad."

The second condition was that all those who had the Lord's feet in their hearts would surely get liberation. The Lord agreed to this also.

The third and last condition of the almost petrified *Gayāsura* was, "If even a single person having the Lord's feet in his heart fails to get liberation, then this petrified *Gayāsura* will again become a living *Gayāsura*." Lord *Viṣṇu* agreed to it. Very soon *Gayāsura* was turned completely into stone.

This story, from one of the *Purānas* [ancient scriptures] has the following three lessons for humanity. First, the Lord will seat Himself in the heart of the devotee without bothering Himself about the nature of that person, good, or bad. It is enough to be a devotee, in order to have the Lord inside. Second, all those who have the Lord's feet in their hearts are bound to get liberation -- liberation is a sure guarantee for them. Third, since *Gayāsura* had been turned to stone by the Lord, and since He would again arise if anyone having the Lord inside failed to be liberated, the Lord would have to grant liberation to all such persons for all time to come; it is a matter of the Lord's prestige!

VIRTUE AND VICE

Virtue and vice are temporal entities. These things have nothing to do with a man's relationship with the Supreme Father. Suppose several boys are moving along a road and a boy falls into the drain. His clothes and his body become dirty. Other people, passers-by, will laugh at him, but when the father sees his boy in that condition, what will he do? Will he laugh at his own son? No, no, no. What will he do? He himself will go there into the drain and take his boy in his own lap and clean his clothes, clean his body and after that, he will say, "My boy, you should walk carefully." Sinners are just like that boy in the drain. Clear?

Now, high or low, upgraded or degraded, all are equal for Him because the heaven is His creation, the hell is His creation. If we say that He is only in heaven, it will not be a correct utterance, because He is in hell also. His sons, His daughters are never alone; He is with you even in hell. What should you do? You should always remember that you are the child of a Great Father. You must not think that you are a sinner, that you are a degraded person. If you think that you are a sinner, it means you are meditating on sin. And when sin becomes the object of your meditation, actually you will become a sinner, because a man becomes just like his object of ideation, his object of meditation. If you always meditate on sin, "I am a sinner...I am a sinner..." actually you will become a sinner. The psychological approach is to forget it, even if you are actually a sinner. You should think, "I am the son of a Great Father...I am the son of a Great Father...I am the son of a Great Father," and thus you are meditating on the Great Father. And a day is sure to come when you will become one with your Great Father. But to think, "I am a sinner...I am a sinner...I am a sinner...Oh Father, save me...Oh Father save me...Oh Father, save me..." is a defective approach. You should say, "I am your son...I am your son...Oh Father, take me on your lap, I am your son...I am your son..." This should be the approach. You should forget what you do not want.

Now, wherever there is an expression, or wherever there is no expression, the Witnessing Entity is there; just like the light of a stage, a theatrical stage. When there is an actor the light is there, witnessing the activities of the actor. The actor says something or recites something, and the light of the stage witnesses the activities of that actor. When a singer comes, that same light witnesses the activity of the singer. When a dancer comes, that very light witnesses the activity of that dancer. And when nobody is present -- no actor, no dancer, no singer -- that very light witnesses that nobody is present here now. It expresses the fact before the audience, before the spectators, that there is nobody on the stage. Similarly, where there is expression, that Cosmic Light, that Cosmic Father is there. And where there is no expression, that Cosmic Father is there to say that nobody is present now -- just like that light of the theatrical stage.

The divinity of the human being is sleeping, is in latent form in the last bone of the spine. That latent divinity, that sleeping divinity is called *Kúlakuńdálinii* in Sanskrit, or "coiled serpentine" in English. It is just like a serpentine loop. Now, by means of *sádhana* -- what is *sádhana*? Whenever a *sádhaka* gets his own peculiar incantation, own *mantra*, from his *ácárya* [spiritual teacher], that sleeping divinity, *Kúlakuńdálinii*, is aroused by the vibration of that *mantra*. And by his constant practice, regular practice, that *Kúlakuńdálinii* moves upward. Its original residence is in the *Múládhára cakra*, the lowermost *cakra* [psychic energy center]. Now, when the *sádhaka*, by his *sádhana*, intuitional practice, raises that *Kúlakuńdálinii*, and when the *Kúlakuńdálinii* crosses the *Svádhisthána cakra*, the next higher *cakra*, his feelings, his expressions, his status is known as *sálokya*. It is the first stage of *samádhi*. By constant practice a *sádhaka* is sure to attain that status. But you know, the *Yogis* say that a *sádhaka* cannot attain this status without the special favor of the spiritual *Guru*. This stage is called *sálokya*. In *sálokya*, the *sádhaka* feels that in the stratum where he is, in the sphere where his exalted mind is, he is not alone. The Supreme Father is also with him. This gives him very much pleasure. This first pleasure is called *sálokya samádhi.*

Then when this coiled serpentine, sleeping divinity, crosses the *Maṅipúra cakra,* the controlling point of the pancreas, the *sádhaka* enjoys another sort of pleasure called *sámipya samádhi. Sámipya* means "proximity." That is, he feels his proximity to the Supreme Father. In the first stage he felt that the Supreme Father was with him, in the same status. He is not in the sky. He is everywhere. He is with you. If you are here and He is in the sky, then you are alone here and He is also alone there. No, no, no, no. In the first stage, the feeling was that, "Where I am, He is also with me." And in the second stage, it is, "I have come very close, very near that Supreme Father, I am in close proximity to that Supreme Progenitor. By my *sádhana* the gap between my Father and myself is being reduced." That is the second stage, known as *sámipya. Sámipya* means "proximity."

And when that sleeping divinity, that *Kúlakundalini* crosses the *Anáhata cakra,* the solar plexus in Latin, the *sádhaka's* feelings are known as *sáyuja. Sáyuja* means "in close contact, just side by side, just touching." In the first stage, *sálokya,* he is with you; in the second stage, *sámipya,* you feel the proximity, nearness; and here in *sáyuja,* you feel the tactual experience.

Then, when by your *sádhana* the divinity, the sleeping divinity crosses this point [the throat, location of *Vishuddha cakra*], then one will experience another sort of *samádhi*, a subtler *samádhi*, and that one is called *sárupya*. In *sárupya*, the feeling is "I am one with Him." Not close contact, but oneness. "I am one with the Supreme Progenitor, with the Supreme Cognition." *Sárupya*.

Then, by still more *sádhana*, when this sleeping divinity crosses this point, the controlling point of the pituitary gland, the *A'jiṇa cakra*, the *sádhaka's* experiences are known as *sársthi*, a still higher state. In that point, the feeling is that "I am He." "I" and "He", these two entities have become one. "I am"; but "He" and "I" have coincided. "I", "He". There is one gap. "I am the Supreme Entity." There is the connecting link, "am"; but when "I" and the "Supreme Entity" coincide, this gap, the connecting "am", will disappear. "I" becomes one with "He". Or, "He" becomes one with "I". This stage is called *sársthi*.

And the last stage is when that *Kúlakuńdálini* comes to the seat of *Paramapuruśa*, the controlling point of the pineal gland. The sleeping divinity is to be raised here: this is the final stage of *samádhi*. That final stage of *samádhi* is called *nirvikalpa samádhi* in *Yoga* and *kaevalya* in *Tantra*. *Kevala* means "only", and the noun of *kevala* is *kaevalya*. That is, only one entity exists. That entity may be "I", that entity may be "He", but the differentiation between "I" and "He" disappears. So "I exist" or "He exists" -- these two ideas disappear. Exists. This is the stage of non-attributional consciousness. It is the Supreme stage of *Yogic sádhana*. It is the Supreme Stance of a *Yogi*.

Now, by *sádhana*, one is to arouse and raise that sleeping divinity. But for this, one requires divine help, and I know one is sure to get divine help. And I know further that one is getting divine help. And I know still further, that in future, for infinite time and infinite space, one will be getting this divine favor. And you are all *sádhakas*, you will certainly attain that Supreme Stance and enjoy that Divine Blessedness. You are sure to enjoy it, my sons and my daughters. ○

GOD

To a man of average intelligence, water and ice are two different entities, but he who knows a little of truth knows that ice is only a crudified form of water. Similarly, where the average man sees a big difference between a pot and the potter, the knower of God sees only oneness among them. Are the world and God two different entities or are they indivisible? Is the one true, and the other false? Is the difference that appears between the two the truth, or illusion? Such questions or ways of thinking never arise in the mind of a person with Cosmic outlook.

Whether the world and God are two entities, or the one is not different from the other -- such thoughts are wrong in themselves. The knower of God feels that the world is indeed His own manifestation. He knows that all is He. Do you know how that difference looks from the Cosmic perspective? Not any more than the difference between man and human being, between sea and ocean. From a *sádhakas* standpoint the distinction does not exist.

God is like a person whose surname is [Smith]. The son calls him "father" for he sees in him the father-like manifestation; his father calls him "son" for he sees in him the son-like manifestation; a schoolboy calls him "sir" for he sees in him the teacher-like manifestation; and a rickshaw puller calls him, "Hey, top hat," for he sees his top hat as the all-important thing. But in reality are all these addresses like "father", "sir", or "Hey, top hat!" so many different persons? Actually these are the results of looking at the same person from different angles of vision.

○

God is the Lord of the evolved objects; He is the controller of every one of them. This very Lord moves in the womb as the embryo and when it is born, the event, in fact, should be called the birth of God because all creations are but the manifestations of God Himself.

There is one moon, but its reflections, falling in countless puddles of water, appear as countless moons. No new moon is born. The same moon is being reflected, or is having births, in many receptacles. Similarly, the one and the same God is being manifested as limitless unit entities in countless mental receptacles.

○

The union of a *sádhaka* with God has been expressed with an excellent example. A river, giving up its name and identity, completely merges in the sea and thereafter cannot maintain its own existence except as the sea. Similarly, a *sádhaka*, after merging himself in God, can no longer think of himself except as God. Seeing the Ganges River we can tell that it is the water of the Ganges. We can tell the water of the Yamuna River, or the water of the Sarasvati River, but once they merge in the sea, we cannot separate them, nor can we distinguish the one from the other. Nevertheless they are all there. They all have lost their respective name-entities in the entity of the sea.

When a knower of Truth merges in the Supreme Being, his petty sense of existence loses itself, and attaining unity with the Supreme Entity, he becomes Supreme himself. Spiritual practice is the means for the expansion of the soul, not for its annihilation; so *samádhi* does not mean suicide but self-transcendence. He who has known God becomes God Himself, for the unit entity takes on the very form of his object of ideation. He who has God as his object of ideation, becomes God Himself.

If a salt doll goes to fathom the sea, it will certainly melt and become the sea itself. Similarly, if the knower of God goes to fathom God, he merges in the sea of God and becomes God Himself. Be constantly absorbed in the thought of God and you too will become God. O

THE ESSENCE OF SPIRITUALITY

The essence of *dharma*, spirituality, is hidden in *guhá*. There are several meanings of *guhá* in Sanskrit. One indicates the cave wherein God resides. It is unwise to leave the world, to leave service to humanity and go to the Himalayas to attain *Paramapuruśa*. Well! This universe itself is *Paramapuruśa* -- where will you go by leaving it? In the world one thinks that he is not able to concentrate his mind because of the din and bustle; but in the cave of the Himalayas one thinks that he cannot get sweet fruit in a particular jungle, and hence tomorrow he will be going to pick ripe plums two or three miles away in a different forest. In either of the places one is not free. If *Paramapuruśa* does not want you to know Him, then you will not be able to attain Him in either place. If He wishes you to achieve Him, you can get Him here and now. What He sees is your aspiration for Him. Remember it -- that at every step of your life He is testing whether you have been able to arouse love for Him in your mind. He is testing whether you want Him or worldly objects.

The other meaning of *guhá* is "I am", that is, the

essence of *dharma, Paramapuruśa,* is hidden in your own "I-ness". That which is hidden in your own "I-ness" -- is it essential for you to go to the Himalayas in search of it? Do you require the help of a mirror to see your wristwatch on your wrist? No, you will never do that. Likewise, you need not go to the Himalayas in search of *Paramapuruśa,* who is hidden in your own "I-ness". Living in the world, put forth your entire self for the service of society, and then you will attain *Paramapuruśa.*

Why speak of attaining Him in the future? -- you have already attained Him, you are simply not able to see Him. ○

O tranquil sádhaka! *Sádhana is your great bow. Set the arrow of your mind, sharpened with meditation, on this bow. Now inclining your mind toward Him, pluck and twang the string of the bow and pierce your target -- that indestructible Supreme Soul.*

The Supreme Consciousness is there in you as the oil is in the oilseed. Crush the seed through sádhana and you attain Him; separate the mind from Consciousness and you will see that the resplendence of the Supreme Consciousness illuminates your whole inner being. He is there like butter in curd; churn it and He will appear from within. Churn your mind through sádhana and God will appear like butter from curd. He is like a subterranean river in you. Remove the sands of mind and you will find the clear, cool waters within.

THE SOUND OF GOD

In the beginning, there was sound, and the sound was with God, and the sound was God. You know, sound is the subtlest expression, subtler even than light, and that's why the ears are treated as the subtlest organs. Now, these acoustic expressions are of two kinds: one is divine or spiritual acoustic expression, and the other is physical acoustic expression. Sound is physical acoustic expression, and similarly there is spiritual acoustic expression in the divine realm, in the spiritual realm. But in the case of the Non-attributional Entity, in the case of *Nirguña Brahma* [unmanifested consciousness], there is no expression, because *Nirguña* means "where there is no expression". In the case of *Saguña Brahma* [manifested consciousness] and even starting from the Cosmic Nucleus, there is expression, and that expression, until it reaches the physical sphere, is spiritual acoustic expression, spiritual sound.

You know, whenever you think something, you create mental sound. What is thinking? Thinking is mentally speaking. Is it not a fact? You are thinking, "Ah, my visa will expire on such and such a day." Actually you are speaking mentally. Mmmmmm. And when you speak, others can also hear; when you speak mentally, others may or may not hear. [Much laughter among disciples.]

Now one may catch this physical sound according to the capacity of one's acoustic organs, one's ears. You cannot catch very short or very long sounds. Similarly in the inner sphere there are several stages, several strata, several phases; when the inner senses develop by dint of *sádhana* one will hear that divine sound, that inner sound. It is known as the sound of silence. What? The sound of silence. It is known as the *Om* sound in Sanskrit. *Pranava* or the *Om* sound.

When these inner senses develop, then in the first phase the *sádhaka* [meditator] can hear that inner sound, that inner voice, that divine sound. In the first phase it is like the sound of crickets. You know, the cricket is an insect which creates a pauseless sound in the open fields, particularly in the rainy season. Mmmm...one will hear cricket sound. Then in the next phase, as if somebody is dancing with ankle bells. Then in the next phase, one will hear the sound of flutes, as if somebody is playing the flute. Then, the sound of the ocean. . .and then, in the fifth stage: tung, tung, just like bells, the sound of bells. And finally, the sound is just like: AAUUUMMM -- the *Om* sound in pure form. And after that there remains no sound because after that realm, after the scope of *Saguña Brahma*, there is the scope of

Nirguña. In the realm of *Nirguña* there can be no sound because there can be no expression. Not even divine expression, not even supra-psychic expression.

By dint of *sádhana*, in the last phase you will hear the sound, the *Om* sound -- AAUUMMM. You will hear that sound. In the *Vedas* [spiritual scriptures] it is said, *"Pranava átmakaṁ Brahma"* -- *Pranava* means that entity that helps the *sádhaka* to come in contact with *Paramapuruśa*. In Sanskrit, another name for *Pranava* is *Shabda Brahma* -- *Brahma* expressed as sound. When one can hear that *Pranava*, in the next phase one will come in contact with *Nirguña Brahma*.

So the day will come when this *Pranava* will become a reality for you. Now, for some of you, *Pranava* is in dreamland. [Much laughter of disciples.] ○

DESIRE AND DEVOTION

In the process of evolution, in the movement from crude to subtle, there is one tendency: with the association of the enjoyable object there is a desire to obtain it. You must remember this. For instance, a man living in town has clothes and living conditions according to the dress and housing of the urban people, and when living in a village he has them according to the villagers. This is because of the desire arising out of his association with the people in the town and in villages, respectively. When some persons take tea, you also have a desire to do the same.

In this cosmic cycle [*Brahmacakra*] everyone has his individual and particular desire, and everyone is running after it. Those who have several desires run after all of them and become exhausted; and in the long run they receive none. Those who have only one desire fulfill it very easily. Therefore, instead of running after several objects, run after God and catch Him, because here there is only one desire. When there is more than one desire the mind is divided and nothing will be achieved.

Humans run after their respective desires either because of inborn instinct or imposed *saṁskáras*, and according to the play of *Prakrti* [creative energy], man has many desires. He runs after them and forgets *Paramapuruśa*, and thus the play [*liilá*] of *Paramapuruśa* goes on. When the movement towards their desires is stopped, men start moving towards the Nucleus of these desires.

Desire creates promptness for action. In no case should man be freed from desire; without desire there will be disturbance. One has only to see the type of the desire. Where there is no desire, existence is annihilated. Since desire is indispensable for the existence of life, a man must see what kind of desire should be made.

It was said above that when a man runs after varieties, he gets none. Sometimes a man thinks of becoming a minister, sometimes a secretary, sometimes a poet. There are a thousand and one desires. Because of this the desire is not fully achieved. A man becomes exhausted after running after material objects and ultimately there is no success in action.

The real action is to move towards *Brahma* [the Supreme Entity] and that action is nothing but another form of *Brahma* -- it is His metamorphosis. Hence, taking action to be *Brahma,* go on performing actions. The action which you will do in that stage will have the proper desire behind it. And that desire will be only one and not many. In such a case there will be much more acceleration in the process of *pratisaiñcara* [evolution].

As said above, when the desire is single, the work will be done. When there are so many desires, the work will not be done at all. If one desires to drink milk and smoke at the same time, it cannot be done. A man can only do one or the other. Hence the desire should be *Paramapuruśa* and nothing else; the desire for other objects has to be channeled towards *Paramapuruśa*. This will be the right desire; this is love; this is liberation [*mukti*]. The correct desire for men is devotion.

If a man wants to become a devotee of the Lord, but if deep in his mind he thinks that God will make him pass in his examination -- here the desire is not one but two. When something is demanded from God the desire becomes two, and the time will be completely wasted. Where this desire is towards *Paramapuruśa* alone, there it is known as devotion: "I want *Paramapuruśa,* and from Him I want nothing." Where there is devotion there will be success in action and victory for devotees. This world is for devotees and for nobody else. When this desire is not for *Paramapuruśa* but for something else, it is known as attachment and not devotion. Therefore the correct desire is devotion.

This does not mean that the devotee will only sing *bhajan* and *kiirtan*. They are not seasoned devotees! That *sádhaka* who moves speedily on the path of evolution towards *Paramapuruśa* will never be blind to the sufferings of numberless persons around him due to the lack of a solid social system, solid economic system and human feeling. If he is blind to the ill-management of the social system, he has not been able to understand *Paramapuruśa* fully. If he does so, he will have a subjective approach but not objective adjustment; but when a devotee will move towards *Paramapuruśa* his approach will be "salvation for self and service to humanity." He goes on moving towards *Paramapuruśa* while serving humanity. When humanity is neglected, "salvation for self" is also destroyed. Hence the devotee must be ready to serve humanity. The *sádhakas* who do not render social service do not have real devotion. In their devotion lies selfishness. The devotees who are selfish do not attain God. Hence the correct desire is devotion. Those who are devotees are workers. They will never be afraid of work. They will do maximum work.

Now when you go to perform an action, you will have to learn the skill of performing it. Hence there is a need for knowledge. Those who are real devotees will not neglect *karma* [action] and they will also acquire the knowledge necessary to perform real action. Knowledge and action cannot take a devotee to *Paramapuruśa* -- devotion can. But for serving humanity, for objective adjustment, knowledge and action are essential. Devotees will have to learn this.

The more a man nears *Paramapuruśa*, the more meaningful his life becomes. The existence of a crude-minded man is not as valuable; the existence of germs and insects is not as valuable although they too have the feeling of their existence. Everybody's existence does not have the same value. At the death of a certain man everyone weeps, but at the death of another man people feel relieved. By action, knowledge and devotion, existence is made valuable. This alone is true practicality. The more a man's existence merges in *Paramapuruśa*, the more valuable he becomes. The person who does not practice objective adjustment and fails to see the living beings as the Supreme Consciousness, will never reach *Paramapuruśa*. He can never be great.

> *Devotion is that bridge which connects the unit with the Cosmic Consciousness. Before crossing the bridge of devotion one feels, "You are That Supreme Consciousness." But while crossing the bridge, he feels, "I am That."*

People who are self-centered do not have *Paramapuruśa* as their goal. Outwardly they say that *Paramapuruśa* should be attained, but in their inner mind they have the desire for something else. Such people outwardly say that *Paramapuruśa* should be obtained, but in their inner mind they desire fame or riches; they have crude objects as their goal. What the external mind feels is not the goal of the living being; what the inner mind says is the goal. If the goal of the inner mind is a crude object, the consciousness will be transformed into a crude object. This is *jad́a samádhi* [crude *samádhi*]. *Jad́a samádhi* is very far below human existence and it is very difficult to free oneself from that. After millions of years, human life will be achieved. Just see how dangerous it is. So with *Paramapuruśa* do not have two personalities, inside one thing and outside something else. Become the same outside as you are within, or else your entire mental structure, your entire ectoplasmic stuff will be converted into the crude world of the five fundamental factors.

There are also some people who have the correct desire but do not have correct direction. They know that the *Paramapuruśa* is the goal, but they don't have real direction. It is said that spiritual practice should not be performed studying from books. For it, a preceptor is essential. If a man starts doing *sádhana* by reading a book or hearing from another that too is dangerous because in that case a clear conception about the goal is not formed. Hence one does not know where one is going. The boat is sailing but the sailor does not know where the boat is going. In the long run the sailor will become exhausted and have some accident.

In that case when such persons die, the state after death is known as *videhiliina* [mind without body]. Their existence is not finished herein, but their feelings remain abstract in the ideational world. This, too, is as dangerous as *jada samádhi* [crude samádhi]. The difference between *jada samádhi* and *videhiliina* is that in the former there is folly because of the hidden desire; whereas in the latter there is no folly, rather the lack of correct direction.

Hence everyone should know that without direction nothing can be done. Everything should be done with proper direction, proper guidance. People loudly cry, "Revolution! Revolution!" but revolution does not mean setting buses and trains on fire or tearing up railway lines. This causes the government damage, but the government belongs to the people. Therefore this damages the people themselves. All these are destructive approaches. The persons who use such destructive approaches lack knowledge.

Similarly, if some mistake is made in *sádhana*, it is due to lack of knowledge. Because of this, both the individual and the society are harmed. This is *videhiliina*; *videhiliina* is sure to occur if there is no love for *Paramapuruśa*.

A *sádhaka* who has love for *Paramapuruśa* and action and knowledge and who performs *sádhana* and service to humanity, may have a great deal of cosmic ideation and yet still feel duality between *Paramapuruśa* and himself. Then he will enjoy bliss and become temporarily free from miseries. That state of bliss is *bháva samádhi* [ideational trance]. The persons who attain *bháva samádhi* are devotees, but the duality still exists. Everybody is born out of *Paramapuruśa*, so how can there be two -- the devotee and *Paramapuruśa*? Hence in *bháva samádhi* the higher state is not attained. As long as the mind is in *bháva samádhi* there is bliss, but afterwards the aspirant is an ordinary human being again.

Some devotees move farther ahead and feel oneness with Him, but instead of loving *Paramapuruśa* Himself, think more of His qualities [*guńas*]; in such a case they attain a trance of qualities. In that case the devotees also attain so many qualities, but permanent unification with *Paramapuruśa* is not attained. What happens in the trance of qualities is that the devotee has much more of the feeling of the qualities. Secondly, he thinks that his coming in this universe should be justified. He wants to justify his body, mind, soul and whole life. These are sentient feelings indeed -- but these devotees are also not seasoned devotees!

One should have the feeling that the body and mind, which have been given by *Paramapuruśa*, will be utilized in the service of society to please *Paramapuruśa*. Persons who please *Paramapuruśa* are devotees. Their very nature is to please *Paramapuruśa*. Devotees of the first order will not want the trance of qualities. They will want to utilize their bodies, minds and their qualities for the service of humanity, because everything belongs to *Paramapuruśa*. He has expressed Himself into every object of the universe, even to the blade of grass. A devotee will serve the universe because this will please *Paramapuruśa*.

Those persons who utilize themselves fully to please *Paramapuruśa* are Class A devotees. They alone are devotees and the others are not. Where the only aim is to please *Paramapuruśa*, there the devotee completely forgets himself, because self-centeredness is pleasing oneself. Up to the trance of qualities even this sense of self-centeredness exists. But where there is no personal desire and the only aim is to please *Paramapuruśa*, self-centeredness does not exist at all. And in the absence of self-centeredness, the final merger of existence occurs. With the extinction of existence, the Absolute Consciousness is established. Everything is done for the happiness of *Shiva*, of *Paramapuruśa*. This establishment of *Shiva* consciousness is known as *Shiva samádhi*. The Supreme Goal of human life is *Shiva samádhi*. People become established in *Shiva samádhi* by "salvation for self and service to humanity." There is no other way out.

It may be questioned how an illiterate, weakling man will do action and acquire knowledge. There is only one answer to this. If one is a devotee then *Paramapuruśa* will teach him the technique of rendering services.

> Devotion is service to God
> Devotion is love personified
> Devotion is the form of Bliss
> Devotion is the life of the devotee.

Devotion is service to God; devotion is to please the Lord and not to please any worldly object. Devotion is love personified. The man who does not have compassion, the man who does not shed tears at the miseries of others, is not a man but a stone. He cannot do any great work. Be happy with the happiness of others and troubled with the trouble of others. This alone is natural. Do not be unnatural. The effort to make everybody one's own culminates in love for the Lord -- devotion is love-for-God personified.

Devotion is the ecstasy of bliss, the ocean of bliss. And devotion alone is the life for the devotee. The greatest hostility against devotees is to take away their devotion. Do not ever try to snatch devotion from devotees since devotion is their life.

Paramapuruśa himself will teach knowledge and the technique of doing the work. It is not the devotees' headache. Surrender everything to the Lord. Because a man has not been able to solve his problem by his efforts, nor will he be able to, still a devotee must not be disturbed. If one requires something from God, one must ask only for absolute devotion. When devotion is attained, God is attained. If God is attained, everything is attained. What remains unattained!?

Therefore, from ancient times learned people have been accepting that the wisest man in the world is the devotee. The devotee is not bereft of intellect. On the contrary he is the wisest. If you want to remain in the world, remain like a devotee. As long as devotion is not there, one's heart is like a desert; and when devotion is attained, an oasis appears in the desert.

You do not have to be afraid of anything when devotion is with you. There is nothing to be afraid of when *Paramapuruśa* is with you. When devotion is there, *Paramapuruśa* is there. And when He is there, fear none. In no case need you feel disturbed.

You must remember that devotion is a unique creation of *Paramapuruśa*. And remembering this, learning, intellect, money are not at all needed. Ask and you will get the cheapest but the most invaluable treasure.

Hence be a devotee and establish the Ideology. If devotion is with you, whatever you want, in whatever way you want, you will establish your Ideology. Those who are devotionless will go on blinking and can never do anything against you.

If devotion is with you, victory is with you. ○

That which makes the mind soft and strong and strenuous, so it may keep itself in a balanced state even in the condition of pain, that which perpetually creates a pleasant feeling within is called love. Devotion is identical with love. The moment devotion is aroused, the love of God comes.

THE CLARION CALL OF THE UNIVERSAL

O human beings! You are fortunate. The clarion call of the Universal has reached you. That very call is vibrating in every cell of your body. Will you now lie inert in the corner of your house? Will you now waste your time by clutching ancient skeletons to your breast and moaning over them? The Supreme Being is calling you in the roar of the ocean, in the thunder of the clouds, in the speed of the lightning, in the meteor's flaming fires. Nothing will come of remaining idle. Get up and awaken the clouded chivalry of your dormant youth. The path may not be strewn with flowers -- an inferiority complex may seek to hold back your every advancing footstep, but even then you have to proceed onward, tearing the shroud of darkness. You will soon rend the thick darkness of despair on the way to the attainment of the Supreme State, and advance onwards in the swift-moving chariot, radiant with the sun's brilliance. O

*Departing Message
From The Philippines*

*Now I am leaving this country and I am leaving you physically. I am always with you; I will always be with you. Physically I am leaving you, my sons and daughters, but I can't forget you, and mentally I will always be with you. I want all of you to be ideal human beings. All of you should attain the pinnacle of human glory. Let your existence be successful. I have nothing more to say. Peace be with you. My sons and daughters, I have one more sentence to say. I do not belong to heaven. What I am, I am to express this truth in a single sentence --
I am yours.*

SURRENDER

Lord *Krṣṅa* says, "My *Máyá*, the force that creates confusions and distinctions, is very powerful; it is insurmountable by the unit minds. But those who surrender unto Me, transcend these forces of Mine with My help."

If *Máyá* is more powerful than unit beings, will the sons of God remain forever slaves of this force? Is there no hope? No. This situation is becoming neither of God, nor of His sons.

The secret lies in the word "Mine." "This blinding force, *Máyá*, is Mine; I have used it for the play of My creation. Being Mine, it is within My control to withdraw it from all or any," says the Lord. "Hence those who surrender to Me can easily surmount this force."

But what is the correct way to surrender? Prayer? Asking God for this and for that? There the responsibility for what you ask is yours -- you might ask for something very inferior, although you approach the All-Powerful for it. The best prayer is, therefore, "O Lord! Do whatever you think fit and best for me. I do not know in which way lies my good -- You know."

There was a demon who prayed that he would die neither during the day nor at night. God granted the prayer and he was killed at sunset! Do not be foolish like this. As long as you pray, you are not surrendering, for you are requesting something for yourself. You are looking after yourself.

God can remove *Máyá* from all, at one stroke. He has the power to do so. But that will finish His whole *liila* [pláy] and this drama of creation. Therefore He removes it from individuals, and not from all collectively.

For the good of human society, *sádhakas* will tell others also about the method of this surrender and make them men and women of God. Individual progress depends upon social environment also, and hence the need for *pracár* [spiritual propagation].

Both *sádhana* and success are within your easy reach. The result is already secured with me; I shall give it to you at the appropriate time. Do not bother about it.

Whether you are sinner or virtuous, those who come to God are all one for Him. He makes no distinctions. All will be liberated.

You are all my beloved sons and daughters. Sometimes I appear harsh to some. But that is for love. If I were indifferent, there would be no need for scolding or punishment.

I want to see you all laugh. It gives me great pleasure to see you laughing.

Leave all cares unto me.

O be blessed.

GLOSSARY

Sanskrit words appear in italics in the text. In Roman Sanskrit, a is pronounced as in up; *á as in* father; *e as in* say; *aṁ as* ung; *c as* ch; *ś as* sh; *and* jiṇá *as* gyá.

ÁCÁRYA -- *spiritual teacher; literally, "one who teaches by his conduct and character"*

ADHARMA -- *movement towards imperfection; literally, "not-dharma", not the true nature of man*

ÁNANDA -- *Supreme Bliss*

ÁNANDA MÁRGA -- *the Path of Bliss*

ASAT -- *the transitory; literally, "not-Truth"*

ASAKTHI -- *attraction for the finite material world*

ÁSANA -- *a part of Yogic practice, physical exercises which harmonize the glandular system and thus make the body perfectly fit for meditation*

AVIDYÁ -- *the force leading towards "crudeness", degeneration*

BALA -- *spiritual force*

BALVÁN -- *full of spiritual force*

BHAJAN -- *devotional song*

BHAKTI -- *devotion, intense attraction for the Supreme*

BRAHMA -- *God, Cosmic Consciousness*

BRAHMACAKRA -- *the cycle of Brahma, the movement of creation away from God, from the "subtle" to the "crude", from consciousness to matter, and then from the crude to the subtle, back to Him again*

BRAHMA LOKA -- *the realm of Pure Consciousness, subtlest realm of the universe*

CAKRA -- *a psychic and spiritual energy center in the human being; there are seven cakras located along the spinal column*

DAGDHABIIJA -- *"burnt seed", one who surrenders his mind to God and so creates no more saḿskáras, mental reactions*

DHARMA -- *nature, duty, the essential characteristic of an entity*

FIVE FUNDAMENTAL FACTORS -- *the five basic factors from which the material realm of the universe is created: ether, air, fire* (luminous), *liquid, and solid.*

GUŃAS -- *the three binding forces of Prakrti*

GURU -- *spiritual preceptor, literally, "dispeller of darkness"*

HANUMÁN -- *the giant monkey, devoted servant of Ráma (the God-king hero of the Indian epic Rámáyana)*

IISHVARA -- *God; literally, "the controller"*

JIṊÁNA -- *knowledge*

JIṊÁNI -- *man of knowledge*

KARMA YOGA -- *the Yoga of action; actions performed without attachment to the results*

KIIRTAN -- *chanting the Lord's name*

KRŚŃA -- *great Yogi who lived about 3500 years ago in India, still worshipped by millions as a perfectly realized one*

KÚLAKUŃD́ALINI -- *"coiled serpentine", the latent spiritual energy in each human being*

LIILÁ -- *the divine play, the game of God in creating the universe*

MADHUVIDYÁ -- *literally, "honey knowledge", the sweet ideation that God is everywhere, that He is doing everything*

MAHÁBHARATA -- *an Indian epic*

MAHÁYOGI -- *a great Yogi*

MANANA -- *literally, "thinking", thinking about God*

MÁYÁ -- *the Operative Principle, the creative energy of the universe, sometimes called Prakrti*

MOKŚA -- *salvation, the merger of the mind into unqualified Cosmic Consciousness, Nirguńa Brahma*

MUKTI -- *liberation; the merger of the mind into qualified Cosmic Consciousness, Saguńa Brahma*

MUTATIVE FORCE -- *rajoguńa, one of the three guńas or binding forces of Prakrti; causes movement, activity, restlessness*

NAMASKÁR -- *salutations*

NIRGUŃA BRAHMA -- *unmanifested Cosmic Consciousness*

PARAMAPURUŚA -- *the Cosmic Consciousness, God*

PRACÁR -- *the propagation of spiritual practices and philosophy*

PRAKRTI -- *the Operative Principle of God, the Cosmic Energy, sometimes called "MÁYÁ"*

PRÁŃA -- *the vital energy of an entity*

PRANAVA -- *the Om-sound, the sound of God*

PRÁŃAYÁMA -- *a Yogic practice involving control of breath or vital energy*

PREMA -- *divine love*

PREYA -- *material gain*

PURÁNAS -- *ancient Indian mythological scriptures*

RÁMA -- *the mythological God-king, hero of the Indian epic Rámáyana*

RÁMÁYANA -- *an Indian epic story of the victorious battle of the God-king Ráma with the demon-king, Rávana*

RAJOGUŃA -- *the mutative force, one of the three guńas or binding forces of Prakrti, which causes restless activity*

RASALIILÁ -- *the play of God's flow, the rhythmic, vibrational dance of creation, the play of waves in God's ocean*

RÁVANA -- *the demon-king, enemy of Lord Ráma in the Rámáyana*

RUDRA -- *God, literally, "He who makes others weep" in pain and joy*

SAT -- *Truth, the eternal*

SÁDHAKA -- *a spiritual aspirant, practitioner of Yoga*

SÁDHANA -- *meditation, spiritual practice; literally, "effort" or "completion"*

SAGUŃA BRAHMA -- *manifested Cosmic Consciousness*

SAMÁDHI -- *to become one with God, to expand one's unit mind by ideation on God until it merges in God's mind; a state of peace and bliss. Literally, "to become one with the goal"*

SAMSKÁRA -- *the potential reaction of one's action*

SENTIENT FORCE -- *that force of the Cosmic Energy, Prakrti, which causes peace, awareness, self-knowledge, and which leads to liberation*

SEVA -- *service*

SHÁSTRAS -- *scriptures*

SHRAVANA -- *literally, "hearing" about God, telling stories about God and singing His Name*

SHREYA -- *spiritual gain*

STATIC FORCE -- *that force of the Cosmic Energy, Prakrti, which creates inaction, inertia, death*

TAPAH -- *selfless service*

VIŚŃU -- *the all-expanded, all-pervasive Entity, God*

YOGA -- *literally, "unification", the union of the unit consciousness with the Supreme Consciousness, of the spiritual aspirant with God*

YOGI -- *one who has achieved God-realization*

Other books from ANANDA MARGA PUBLICATIONS:
TEACHING ASANAS, An Ananda Marga Manual for Teachers
THE GREAT UNIVERSE, Discourses on Society by Shrii Shrii Anandamurti

*The word
Bábá comes from
Sanskrit. It means
"beloved". For the living
beings, the Lord is the beloved
one,* Bábá nám kevalam. *But for
the Lord, the living being is His
Bábá!* When living beings sing
Bábá nám kevalam, *then
the Lord also sings*
Bábá nám kevalam
in His mind.